Passport to French

CHARLES BERLITZ

Travel Information Supplied
by David Butwin

A SIGNET BOOK

NEW AMERICAN LIBRARY

TIMES MIRROR

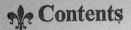 # Contents

Travel Information 1

Preface 7

How to Acquire an Instant French Accent 9

1. Greetings and Introductions *11*
2. Basic Expressions *13*
3. Numbers *16*
4. Arrival *19*
5. Hotel—Laundry—Dry Cleaning *25*
6. Time: Hours—Days—Months *33*
7. French Money *37*
8. Basic Foods *39*
9. Food Specialties of France *47*
10. Transportation *51*
     Bus 51
     Taxi 52
     Subway 54
     Train 56
     Ship 58
11. Trips by Car *61*
     Car Rental 61
     Gas Station 62
     Asking Directions 63
     Emergencies and Repairs 65
     International Road Signs 70
12. Sightseeing and Photography *73*
13. Entertainment *81*
     Things to Do 81
     Theaters and Nightclubs 83
     An Invitation to Dinner 84
14. Talking to People *87*
15. Words That Show You Are "With It" *101*

16. Shopping *105*
        Names of Shops 105
        General Shopping Vocabulary 106
        Clothes 109
        Sizes—Colors—Materials 111
        Newsstand 113
        Tobacco Shop 113
        Drugstore 114
        Cosmetics 114
        Hairdresser 115
        Barber 115
        Food Market 116
        Jewelry 117
        Antiques 118
17. Telephone *119*
18. Post Office and Telegrams *123*
19. Seasons and the Weather *125*
20. Doctor and Dentist *127*
21. Problems and Police *133*
22. Housekeeping *135*
23. A New Type of Dictionary *141*

⚜ Travel Information

Americans have been rediscovering France ever since Ben Franklin, serving as an envoy, made Paris his domain at the end of the eighteenth century. Of course most Americans don't fit into French life as thoroughly as did Mr. Franklin, and somehow many carry away the impression that the French simply don't like Americans. The truth is that the French, or at any rate the Parisians, don't particularly warm up to outlanders of any stripe who insist on asserting their own habits and customs while on Gallic soil. Can you blame them? Once rid of this widely broadcast paranoia, however, travelers should find France an enchanting land. Another overstated travel maxim is that France is too expensive to contend with. This is true of certain restaurants and hotels of Paris, but with a little thought and care France can be seen cheaply—and without starving.

Where to Stay

In France, depending on your mood and resources, you can sleep for less than $1 at grassy campsites and cold-water pensions—or put out $250 for a night in the Empire Suite of the Paris Ritz. Each year, of course, millions of tourists settle for accommodations somewhere between those extremes. Two French offices, the Syndicats d'Initiative and the Bureaux d'Accueil, can open many of the right doors. The syndicats, sometimes known as the Office of Tourism but usually identified only as S.I., provide general *bienvenue,* and their multilingual staffs will furnish room listings and sometimes call ahead to see if rooms are available. The bureaux will do the same and also book rooms without a fee in any corner of France you indicate.

Several associations have grouped together hotels from different parts of the country to ensure common standards of comfort and cuisine. For instance, the Logis de France et Auberges de Vacances, specializing in lower-priced accommodations, controls 3,000 hotels. The simplest in this group, the auberges, usually outside of town, promise hot and cold running water in all rooms. An annual guide to Logis de France et Auberges de Vacances is available for $2, from the Fédération des Logis de France, 26 rue d'Artois, Paris 8. A choice of 10,000 villas, houses, and apartments can be rented from the Fédération Nationale des Gîtes de France, 34 rue Godot-de-Mauroy, Paris 9. Accommodations are plain, clean, and often part of a Frenchman's home; so you might find yourself sitting down to dinner with his family.

How to Eat

In the land of Escoffier, a visitor can part with $50 at Maxim's, $10 at a café of Fouquet's excellence, or as little as $2 to $3 at a small bistro or restaurant. Whatever you choose, it's always cheaper to opt for the prix fixe menu than to select individual dishes à la carte. Many restaurants offer a *ménu touristique* with appetizer, main dish, cheese, or dessert for $2 or so. Such places are recognized by the menu on the front window or a door affixed with a *restaurant de tourisme* disk.

Nor can you go wrong—or seldom anyway—in one of the countless bistros of Paris or the provinces. You probably won't see a printed menu, the fare depending on the owner's whim or the price of meat that morning in the market. Usually you get a carafe of *vin ordinaire* and the *plat du jour*. Or the chef may prepare his *specialité de la maison*, a dish he learned to cook in his home region.

Other institutions dedicated to the perpetuation of French cuisine, reasonably priced, include the more than fifty *libre-service* Paris restaurants—cafeterias to you—which charge only $1.40 for three courses; *pâtisseries*, sometimes furnished with a few chairs and tables, where you can fill up on coffee, croissants, and other pastries for a few francs; *restoroutes,* or *routiers,* akin to American truck stops, with substantial meals for about $1.50. Of course, in France there isn't a better sidewalk snack than *le sandwich*—small, crisp French bread with either cheese, ham, or liver pâté. You may never go back to hot dogs.

What to Buy

You don't have to shop in the famous couture houses and boutiques along the Faubourg St-Honoré to find high-quality merchandise. Small and more obscure shops may have the same items for much less. You can expect to pay thirty or forty percent less for St. Laurent ready-to-wear; Hermès scarves; Charles Jourdan shoes; Louis Vuitton luggage; the famous scents, Guerlain, Lanvin, Patou; Limoges china; and Baccarat crystal. Lesser-known brand names bring bargains, too. Thanks to the watchful eye of the national tourist office, department stores are reliable in their mailing processes. It is, of course, advisable to insure expensive purchases. You can get a fifteen to twenty percent reduction if you have the patience to fill out a series of forms in the store, leave one with the shopkeeper, and turn over two copies to customs before leaving France for the United States. Any tourist office can fill you in on this procedure. Shoppers are also hereby advised to buy any cloth or fabric labeled Tergal—a process that maintains the neatness and resiliency of dresses, shirts, curtains, or bedspreads. This remarkable process is almost unknown in the United States.

Orly, the Paris international airport, brims with all the big name brands—and duty-free. Corridor kiosks en route to the gates sell cheese in foil, pâté de foie gras, and caviar. In the basement *supermarché* (not duty-free) a departing passenger may buy an armful of the long French breads or—if they arouse your fancy—the very blue French overalls which seem almost a uniform in France.

How to Travel

French trains are perhaps the sleekest and soundest in the world. Few trains anywhere can match the Paris-Nice Le Mistral. Christened in 1950, Le Mistral packs a newsstand, Articles de Paris boutique, a barber shop and beauty salon, dens complete with dictating equipment and ready secretaries, and of course a gliding restaurant of epic provisions. Le Mistral connects Paris and Nice in nine hours and ten minutes, hitting a top speed of 100 mph. Even faster is the Paris-Toulouse Le Capitole, which tops off at 125.

Although the French rail network fans out all over the country, many of France's glories are better reached by automobile. Car rentals are slightly higher in France than in other European countries because of a high government tax. Avis runs a little cheaper than Hertz, and local agencies may offer varied rates; so a comparison is wise. Some visitors forget they can fly within France, too. Air Inter, the domestic carrier, doesn't offer many frills, but its Caravelles connect the main cities with regular service.

Young hitchhikers find France an unfertile region, at least on the main routes. Off in the less-traveled provinces, the story is different. In Brittany, for example, local hospitality is such that fishermen are often willing to take you out in the Channel if you buy them a glass of the local wine. Another way to get a ride is by dialing P-R-O-Y-O in Paris and signing on with an agency that has a list of cars heading for all points in France and Europe. The agency, with offices at 16 rue de Provence, charges just $2 for registration. For shorter journeys, you can always rent a bicycle at Gruebet, 58 rue Lafayette—$4 for the first day and $2 afterward.

What to Do

The maddening thing about visiting France is that there are so many sights to see, and seldom time enough. If you don't trust your own devices, you can always hire a private guide for $20 to lead you on a three-hour tour, or take a tour bus through the city for $4.50. Lately, a few other travel aides have been established—among them, government-run walking tours (90 cents for adults, 63 cents for students and chilldren). A guide, or *conferencière*, leads small parties through different parts of Paris each day, Monday through Saturday; place of departure varies, though all leave at 3:00 P.M. The tours take in such places as "The Cradle of Paris: Ile de la Cité and Notre Dame." You can write to Mme Bernadette Alambret, Chef du Service des Relations Extérieures, Caisse Nationale des Monuments Historiques, Hôtel de Sully, 62 rue Sainte-Antoine, Paris 4.

Outside of Paris, the budget-conscious tourist of necessity steers away from the Riviera. But this glittering coastal region, called "the most beautiful country in the world" by Renoir, should not be ignored on financial considerations alone. A car can be rented for about $7.50 a day, motor scooters run $4 daily, and the bus and train service between towns is fast and cheap. If you watch the menus carefully, a $2 meal can be found in Côte d'Azur restaurants. Local specialties include *bouillabaisse, salade Niçoise,* and *loup de mer*—a fish, literally, "wolf of the sea."

Generally, as you head west from the Riviera life grows simpler and less expensive, and such uncelebrated towns as Collioure, the ancient fortress of Carcassonne, and the city of Albi (home of Toulouse-Lautrec) provide tourists with the rare feeling of discovery. Carcassonne, its gray turreted towers rearing into the broad Languedoc sky, draws its share of visitors, but few Americans among them. Somehow, a $6 room can be had at the stately ivy-clad Hôtel de la Cité, and $1.80 to $4.40 will cover a full lunch at one of the city's half-timbered *crêperies*.

Northwest from Paris, the province of Brittany also beckons with reasonable rates. Vannes, Lorient, Quimperlé, and Quimper are all pleasantly off the trail, rooms renting for as low as $2, and seafood meals of crab, crayfish, and oysters costing even less. All in all, it's one of the few $5-a-day regions left in France.

Tourists can't seem to get enough of the Loire Valley. Known as the garden of France, the Loire Valley is watered not only by the Loire itself but also by the Cher, Indre, and Vienne rivers. It has been described as a Mason-Dixon Line dividing the north and south. In the north are Paris, progress, and prosperity; in the south are olive and orange groves, mulberry trees crawling with silkworms, the Basque country, and the beaches of Cannes and Nice. Levees and dikes—some built centuries ago—butt into the Loire at various points to hold back the water.

About an hour and a half by train out of Paris's Gare d'Austerlitz you reach Orléans and the beginning of château country. Tours, the seat of the region and site of a famous cathedral, is about two and a half hours away. Bus tours circle the château country, departing from all its major cities. You can make the rounds by car in two or three days, but a week would be better.

Amboise, built mainly by Italian artisans, was the some-time home of Leonardo da Vinci. He is said to be buried in its Gothic chapel of St. Hubert. For little more than half a dollar you can take in its Gothic and Renaissance architecture, and period pieces like Aubusson tapestries, mullioned windows, and fifteenth-century furniture. Blois, begun in the thirteenth century, is a huge, parapeted castle that looks down on the gray slate roofs of the old city. It was here that Henry III's guards assassinated Henri de Lorraine, duc de Guise, and Catherine de' Medici also died here in 1589. In one room are the secret panels where she concealed assorted potions and poisons. Chenonceaux, an architectural classic, was begun in 1513 and later inhabited by Diane de Poitiers, mistress of Henry II while he was married to Catherine de' Medici. Among the appointments are some Rubens originals.

DAVID BUTWIN

NOTE: *Prices in dollars will vary according to whatever rate of exchange is in effect at a given time.*

⚜ Preface

Is it possible to learn to speak French from a phrase book? If one means basic communication—the ability to speak, understand, and generally get along—the answer is "yes," *if* you learn the right phrases. The secret of learning languages is to learn not only individual words, but the phrases in which they are apt to occur on a frequency basis—as the French use them every day.

The purpose of this book is to provide instant communication in French. The phrases are short, geared to situations of daily life, and pinpointed for easy reference so that you can find the exact section you need at any moment.

There is even a chapter—"Words That Show You Are 'With It'"—that gives you the key words and phrases that French people use to add color to their conversation. In this way, instead of learning about "the umbrella of my aunt," you learn to use the right phrase at the right time, in the very way a French person would use it. And, so that French people will understand your accent, all you have to do is read the phonetic line under each French phrase *as if it were English*. Further practice and listening to French people speaking will improve your accent.

The use of this book is not limited to a trip to France, Canada, Belgium, Switzerland, or other French-speaking countries. French is spoken throughout the world, and, besides the pleasure and help you will get by speaking French on your travels; you will find it an additional pleasure to use the idiomatic French you will learn in this book in French restaurants and with French-speaking people you may meet anywhere.

Young people studying French in a more conventional manner in school or college will find this book invaluable as an aid to their studies in that it brings modern colloquial French alive as a means of communication.

The use of this book will more than double your

enjoyment of a trip abroad and also help-you save money. Besides the economic factor, why visit a foreign country if you can't break the language barrier and communicate with the new and interesting people you meet? You might as well stay home and see the palaces and monuments of the country on color TV. Why be limited to one language when picking up another language can be so easy and enjoyable?

One can speak and understand current everyday French with comparatively few words and phrases—perhaps 1500 to 1800—which is less than the number given in the speaking dictionary at the end of this book. By using the same short constructions over and over in the various situations where they normally occur, you will acquire them without conscious effort. They will become a part of your own vocabulary and of your memory bank, and that is, after all, the only "secret" of learning a language.

⚜ How to Acquire an Instant French Accent

Every word or sentence in this book is presented in English, in French, and in easy-to-read phonetics to help you pronounce the French you see. Just pronounce the phonetics as if you were reading English, with the following exceptions:

1. We have expressed the French **u** in the phonetics as *ü*. To make this sound, pronounce "ee" with your lips rounded in a tight circle as if to whistle. For example, the well known Rue de la Paix is pronounced *rü duh la pay*.

2. The French nasal sound of "n" is expressed by *n*, a signal to stop breathing and say it through your nose.

(English)	No.
(French)	Non.
(Phonetics)	*nohn.*

3. The soft French **j** is expressed by *zh* in the phonetics. This is pronounced like the "s" in "measure."

> I travel a lot.
> Je voyage beaucoup.
> *zhuh vwa-yahzh bo-koo.*

French word linkage is expressed in the phonetics by attaching the "linking" letter to the next word, just as it sounds.

> Where are they?
> Où sont-ils?
> *oo sohn teel?*

---

1. *Pronounce ü like ee with your lips in a tight circle.*
2. *zh is like the s in measure.*
3. *n means a nasal "n," pronounced through the nose.*

French **a** is pronounced like the *a* in the English word *pa*.

French **o** is pronounced like the *o* in the English word *so*.

An additional piece of advice will enable you to sound even more like a true son or daughter of France: French syllables have nearly equal stress, but give a slight additional emphasis to the *last* syllable of every phrase.

> **Paris is my favorite city.**
> Paris est ma ville préférée.
> *pa-ree ay ma veel pray-fay-RAY.*

With this advice and the easy phonetic system we have devised, you will certainly be told:

> **Vous avez un très bon accent!**
> *voo za-vay un tray bohn nak-sahn!*

This means, "You have a very good accent!"

⚜ 1. Greetings and Introductions

When addressing people, call them Monsieur, Madame, Mademoiselle—with or *without* the last name. Even when you say simply Bonjour! ("Good morning!" or "Good day!") it is more polite to add one of these forms of address.

Mr. or Sir	Mrs. or Madam	Miss
Monsieur	Madame	Mademoiselle
muss-yuh	*ma-dahm*	*mahd-mwa-zell*

Good morning (or)
   Good afternoon, sir.
Bonjour, Monsieur.
bohn-zhoor, muss-yuh.

Good evening, madam.
Bonsoir, Madame.
bohn-swahr ma-dahm.

How are you?
Comment allez-vous?
ko-mahn tal-lay-voo?

Very well, thank you. And you?
Très bien, merci. Et vous?
tray b'yen, mair-see. ay voo?

Come in.
Entrez.
ahn-tray.

Sit down, please.
Asseyez-vous, s'il vous plaît.
ah-say-yay-voo, seel voo play.

I am Henry Marchant.
Je suis Henri Marchant.
*zhuh swee ahn-ree
   mahr-shahn.*

What is your name?
Quel est votre nom?
kel ay votr' nohn?

---

1. *Pronounce ù like ee with your lips in a tight circle.*
2. *zh is like the s in measure.*
3. *n means a nasal "n," pronounced through the nose.*

May I introduce . . .
Je vous présente . . .
zhuh voo pray-zahʜt . . .

Delighted (to meet you).
Enchanté.
ahʜ-shahʜ-tay.

Goodbye.
Au revoir.
oh-ruh-vwahr.

Good night.
Bonne nuit.
bunn nwee.

See you soon.
A bientôt.
ah-b'yen-toh.

En passant (by the way): If you do not know whether a lady is married or not, address her as **Madame** rather than **Mademoiselle**. And to kiss a lady's hand is a gesture. of respect toward a married woman.

❧2. Basic Expressions

Learn these by heart. You will use them every time you speak French to someone. If you memorize these expressions and the numbers in the next section, you will find that you can ask prices and directions and generally make your wishes known.

Yes	No	Perhaps	Please	Thank you
Oui	Non	Peut-être	S'il vous plaît	Merci
wee	*nohn*	*puh-tetr'*	*seel voo play*	*mair-see*

You are welcome.	Pardon	I am sorry.
De rien.	Pardon	Je regrette.
duh-r'yen.	*par-dohn*	*zhuh ruh-grett.*

It's all right.	here	over there	this	that
Ça va.	ici	là-bas	ceci	cela
sa va.	*ee-see*	*la-ba*	*suh-see*	*suh-la*

Do you speak English?	I speak French—a little.
Parlez-vous anglais?	Je parle français—un peu.
par-lay voo zahn-glay?	*zhuh parl frahn-say—un puh.*

Do you understand?	I understand.
Comprenez-vous?	Je comprends.
kohn-pruh-nay voo?	*zhuh kohn-prahn.*

I don't understand.	Very well.
Je ne comprends pas.	Très bien.
zhuh nuh kohn-prahn pa.	*tray b'yen.*

1. Pronounce *ü* like *ee* with your lips in a tight circle.
2. *zh* is like the *s* in measure.
3. *n* means a nasal "n," pronounced through the nose.

Speak slowly, please.
Parlez lentement, s'il vous plaît.
.*par-lay lahʀt-mahʀ, seel voo play.*

Repeat, please.
Répétez, s'il vous plaît.
ray-pay-tay, seel voo play.

Write it down.
Écrivez cela.
ay-kree-vay suh-la.

Who is it?
Qui est-ce?
kee ess?

Come in.
Entrez.
ahʀ-tray.

Don't come in.
N'entrez pas.
nahʀ-tray pa.

Stop!
Arrêtez!
ahr-ray-tay!

Wait!
Attendez!
ah-tahʀ-day!

Let's go.
Allons.
ahl-lohʀ.

That's all.
C'est tout.
say too.

What is this?
Qu'est-ce que c'est?
kess kuh say?

Where is the telephone?
Où est le téléphone?
oo ay luh tay-lay-fohn?

Where are the restrooms?
Où sont les lavabos?
oo sohʀ lay la-va-bo?

. . . for ladies.
. . . pour dames.
. . . poor dahm.

. . . for men.
. . . pour
   hommes.
. . . poor ohm.

Show me . . .
Montrez-moi . . .
*moʀ-tray
   mwa . . .*

How much?
Combien?
kohʀ-b'yeʀ?

It's too much.
C'est trop.
say tro.

Who?
Qui?
kee?

When?
Quand?
kahʀ?

How far?
A quelle distance?
ah kel dees-tahnss?

How much time?
Combien de temps?
kohʀ-b'yeʀ duh tahʀ?

How?
Comment?
kom-mahʀ?

Like this.
Comme ça.
kom sa.

Not like that.
Pas comme ça.
pa kom sa.

There it is!
Voilà!
vwa-la!

It is possible.	It is not possible.	Why not?
C'est possible.	Ce n'est pas possible.	Pourquoi pas?
say po-see-bl'.	*suh nay pa po-see-bl'.*	*poor-kwa pa?*

Now.	Not now.	Later.	Really?
Maintenant.	Pas main-	Plus tard.	Vraiment?
meн-tuh-nahн.	tenant.	*plǔ tar.*	*vray-mahн?*
	pa meн-tuh-		
	nahн.		

It's very good.	It's not good.
C'est très bien.	Ce n'est pas bien.
say tray b'yeн.	*suh nay .pa b'yeн.*

En passant: The phrase **S'il vous plaît,** which you should always use when you ask questions or make requests, can also function for "Bring me . . . ," "I want . . . ," or "I would like . . . ," etc. Simply say **S'il vous plaît** followed by the word for whatever you want, which you can find in the dictionary section at the end of this book.

1. *Pronounce ǔ* like *ee* with your lips in a tight circle.
2. *zh* is like the *s* in measure.
3. *н* means a nasal "n," pronounced through the nose.

⚜ 3. Numbers

The numbers are important not only for asking prices (and perhaps to bargain) but for phone numbers, addresses, and telling time. Learn the first twenty by heart and then from 20 to 100 by tens and *voilà!* You have them!

1 un *un*	**2** deux *duh*	**3** trois *trwa*	**4** quatre *katr'*	**5** cinq *senk*
6 six *seess*	**7** sept *sett*	**8** huit *weet*	**9** neuf *nuff*	**10** dix *deess*

11 onze *ohnz*	**12** douze *dooz*	**13** treize *trayz*	**14** quatorze *ka-torz*
15 quinze *kenz*	**16** seize *sayz*	**17** dix-sept *dee-set*	**18** dix-huit *dees-weet*

19 dix-neuf *dees-nuff*	**20** vingt *ven*	**21** vingt et un *vent-ay-un*
22 vingt-deux *vent-duh*	**25** vingt-cinq *vent-senk*	**30** trente *trahnt*
40 quarante *ka-rahnt*	**50** cinquante *senk-ahnt*	**60** soixante *swa-sahnt*
70 (60 and 10) soixante-dix *swa-sahnt-deess*	**71 (60 and 11)** soixante et onze *swa-sahnt ay ohnz*	**80 (4 × 20)** quatre-vingts *katr'-ven*

81 (4 × 20 + 1)
quatre-vingt-un
katr'-vent-un

90 (4 × 20 + 10)
quatre-vingt-dix
katr'-vent-deess

91 (4 × 20 + 11)
quatre-vingt-onze
katr'-vent-ohnz

100
cent
sahn

110
cent dix
sahn deess

200
deux cents
duh sahn

300
trois cents
trwa sahn

a half
un demi
un duh-mee

and a half
et demi (-e)
ay duh-mee

1000
mille
meel

1,000,000
un million
un meel-yohn

100,000
cent mille
'sahn meel

first
premier, première
pruhm-yay, pruhm-yair

second
deuxième
duhz-yem

third
troisième
trwaz-yem

last
dernier, dernière
dairn-yay, dairn-yair

How much? (or) How many?
Combien?
kohn-b'yen?

What number?
Quel numéro?
kel nŭ-may-ro?

En passant: Seventy is formed by the combination "sixty-ten" (soixante-dix), and 71, 72, 73, etc., by combining 60 with 11, 12, 13, and so on, right through the teens: soixante et onze, soixante douze, soixante treize, etc. The same thing happens with 80, which is literally "four twenties"—quatre-vingts, which becomes, for 91, 92, etc., quatre-vingt-onze, quatre-vingt-douze, etc.

---

1. *Pronounce ŭ like ee with your lips in a tight circle.*
2. *zh is like the s in measure.*
3. *n means a nasal "n," pronounced through the nose.*

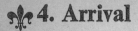# 4. Arrival

Besides exchanging some words with airport officials, one of the most important things you will want to do on arrival in France is to find your way about. For this reason we offer you here some basic "asking your way" questions and answers and call your attention to the "Point to the Answer" sections which the people to whom you speak can use to *point out* answers to make it easier for you to understand.

Your passport, please.
Votre passeport, s'il vous plaît.
votr' pass-por, seel voo play.

I am on a visit.
Je suis de passage.
zhuh swee duh pa-sahzh.

For three weeks.
Pour trois semaines.
poor trwa suh-men.

I am on a business trip.
Je suis en voyage d'affaires.
zhuh swee zahn vwa-yahzh daf-fair.

Where is the customs?
Où est la douane?
oo ay la dwahn?

Where are your bags?
Où sont vos valises?
oo sohn vo va-leez?

My bags are over there.
Mes valises sont là-bas.
may va-leez sohn la-ba.

This one is mine.
Celle-ci est à moi.
sell-see ay ta mwa.

That one.
Celle-là.
sell-la.

---

1. Pronounce *ŭ* like *ee* with your lips in a tight circle.
2. *zh* is like the *s* in measure.
3. *n* means a nasal "n," pronounced through the nose.

Those bags there.
Ces valises-là.
say va-leez-la.

Shall I open it?
Est-ce que je l'ouvre?
ess-kuh zhuh loovr'?

Open it.
Ouvrez-la.
oo-vray-la.

There you are.
Voilà.
vwa-la.

One moment, please.
Un instant, s'il vous plaît.
un nen-stahn, seel voo play.

I am looking for the key.
Je cherche la clé.
zhuh shairsh la clay.

I have nothing to declare.
Je n'ai rien à déclarer.
zhuh nay r'yen na day-kla-ray.

This is for my personal use.
C'est pour mon usage personnel.
say poor mohn û-zahzh pair-sohn-nel.

It has been used.
C'est usagé.
sayt û-za-zhay.

These are gifts.
Ce sont des cadeaux.
suh sohn day ka-doh.

Must I pay something?
Faut-il payer quelque chose?
fo-teel pay-yay kell-kuh-shohz?

Where is the bus to the city?
Où est l'autobus pour la ville?
oo ay lo-toh-buss poor la veel?

Where is a telephone?
Où y a-t-il un téléphone?
oo ee-ya-teel un tay-lay-fohn?

Where is a restaurant?
Où y a-t-il un restaurant?
oo ee-ya-teel un ress-toh-rahn?

Porter!
Porteur!
por-turr

Put these bags into a taxi.
Mettez ces valises dans un taxi.
may-tay say va-leez dahnz un tahk-see.

I'll carry this one myself.
Je porte celle-ci moi-même.
zhuh port sell-see mwa-mem.

How much is it?
C'est combien?
say kohn-b'yen?

To the Hotel de Paris.
À l'Hôtel de Paris.
ah lo-tel duh pa-ree.

To the Hotel Crillon, please.
À l'Hôtel Crillon, s'il vous plaît.
ah lo-tel kree-yohn, seel voo play.

How can I go . . .
Comment peut-on aller . . .
kom-mahn puh-ton al-lay . . .

. . . to a good restaurant?
. . . dans un bon restaurant?
. . . dahn zun bohn ress-toh-rahn?

. . . to the American Consulate?
. . . au consulat américain?
. . . oh kohn-sù-la ah-may-ree-ken?

---

1. *Pronounce* ù *like* ee *with your lips in a tight circle.*
2. *zh is like the* s *in measure.*
3. *n means a nasal "n," pronounced through the nose.*

British	Canadian
britannique	canadien
bree-ta-neek	*ka-nahd-yen*

. . . to the movies?	. . . to this address?
. . . au cinéma?	. . . à cette adresse?
. . . oh see-nay-ma?	*. . . ah set ah-dress?*

. . . to the police station?	. . . to the post office?
. . . au poste de police?	. . . au bureau de poste?
. . . oh post duh po-leess?	*. . . oh bů-ro duh post?*

. . . to the hospital?	. . . to the drugstore?
. . . à l'hôpital?	. . . à la pharmacie?
. . . ah lo-pee-tal?	*. . . ah la far-ma-see?*

. . . to the barber's . . . hairdresser's?
. . . chez le coiffeur?
. . . shay luh kwa-furr?

Follow this street until ——— Street.
Suivez cette rue jusqu'à la rue ———.
swee-vay set rů zhůss-ka la rů ———.

To the right.	To the left.	On the corner.
À droite.	À gauche.	Au coin.
ah drwatt.	*ah gohsh.*	*oh kwen.*

Three streets more.
Encore trois rues.
ahn-kor trwa rů.

Turn left when you get to ———.
Tournez à gauche en arrivant à ———.
toor-nay ah gohsh ahn ar-ree-vahn ah ———.

Follow the Avenue of the Opera.
Suivez l'Avenue de l'Opéra.
swee-vay lav-nů duh lo-pay-ra.

Take bus number ———.
Prenez le Numéro ———.
pruh-nay luh nǔ-may-ro ———.

Is it far?	Yes.	No.
C'est loin?	Oui.	Non.
say lwen?	*we.*	*nohn.*

Take the ——— subway line.
Prenez la ligne ———.
pruh-nay la leen ———.

Thank you very much.	You are very kind.
Merci bien.	Vous êtes très aimable.
mair-see b'yen.	*voo zett trays aim-ahbl'.*

En passant: When you speak to a stranger, don't forget to say **Pardon, Monsieur (or Madame)** before you ask a question. If you talk to a policeman, you can call him **Monsieur** too.

French streets have white-on-blue signs on the buildings at each corner, making it easy to find out where you are.

To make sure you understand people's answers, you can show them the "Point to the Answer" section at the back of the book or the shorter sections in Chapters 5, 8, 10, 11, 12, and 16.

⚜ 5. Hotel—Laundry— Dry Cleaning

Although the staffs of the larger hotels have some training in English, you will find that the use of French makes for better understanding and better relations, especially with the service personnel. Besides, it is fun, and you should practice French at every opportunity. We have included laundry and dry cleaning in this section, as these are subjects about which you have to make yourself understood in speaking to the chambermaid or valet in the hotel.

Can you recommend a good hotel?
Pouvez-vous recommander un bon hôtel?
poo-vay voo ruh-ko-mahn-day un bohn notel?

. . . a guest house?	. . . in the center of town.
. . . une pension?	. . . dans le centre de la ville.
. . . ûne pahns-yohn?	*dahn luh sahntr' duh la veel.*

. . . not too expensive.	I have a reservation.
. . . pas trop cher.	J'ai une réservation.
. . . pa tro shair.	*zhay ûne ray-zair-vahs-yohn.*

. . . in the name of Richard Dupont.
. . . au nom de Richard Dupont.
. . . oh nohn duh ree-shar dû-pohn.

Have you a room?	**I would like a room . . .**
Avez-vous une chambre?	Je voudrais une
ah-vay voo zûne shahnbr'?	chambre . . .
	zhuh voo-dray zûne
	shahnbr' . . .

---

1. *Pronounce û like ee with your lips in a tight circle.*
2. *zh is like the s in measure.*
3. *n means a nasal "n," pronounced through the nose.*

... for one person.
... pour une personne.
... *poor ûne pair-sonn.*

... for two people.
... pour deux personnes.
... *poor duh pair-sonn.*

... with two beds.
... à deux lits.
... *ah duh lee.*

... with a bathroom.
... avec salle de bain.
...*ah-vek sahl duh ben.*

... hot water.
... de l'eau chaude.
... *duh lo shohd.*

... air conditioned.
... climatisée.
... *klee-ma-tee-zay.*

... with a balcony.
... avec un balcon.
...*ah-vek un bahl-kohn.*

... with a radio.
... avec la radio.
... *ah-vek la ra-d'yo.*

... with television.
... avec la télévision.
... *ah-vek la tay-lay-veez-yohn.*

How much is it?   ... per day?   ... per week?
C'est combien?   ... par jour?   ... par semaine?
say kohn-b'yen ... *par zhoor?* ... *par suh-men?*

Are the meals included?
Est-ce que les repas sont compris?
ess kuh lay ruh-pa sohn kohn-pree?

Is breakfast included?
Est-ce que le petit déjeuner est compris?
ess kuh luh puh-tee day-zhuh-nay ay kohn-pree?

I should like to see the room.
Je voudrais voir la chambre.
zhuh voo-dray vwar la shahnbr'.

Where is the toilet?
Où est la toilette?
oo ay la twa-let?

... the shower?
... la douche?
... *la doosh?*

I want another room.	. . . higher up.
Je veux une autre chambre.	. . . plus haut.
zhuh vuh zŭne otr' shahпbr'.	. . . *plŭ oh.*

. . . better.	. . . larger.	. . . smaller.
. . . meilleure.	. . . plus grande.	. . . plus petite.
. . . *may-yurr.*	. . . *plŭ grahпd.*	. . . *plŭ puh-teet.*

I'll take this room.	I'll stay for —— days.
Je prends cette chambre.	Je resterai —— jours.
zhuh prahп set shahпbr'.	*zhuh ress-tuh-ray —— zhoor.*

What time is lunch served?	What time is dinner served?
A quelle heure sert-on le déjeuner?	A quelle heure sert-on le dîner?
ah kel urr sair-tohп luh day-zhuh-nay?	*ah kel urr sair-tohп luh dee-nay?*

I want to be called at 8 o'clock.
Je voudrais qu'on m'appelle à huit heures.
zhuh voo-dray kohп ma-pel ah weet urr.

Bring breakfast to number ——.
Faites monter le petit déjeuner au numéro ——.
fett mohп-tay luh puh-tee day-zhuh-nay
oh nŭ-may-ro ——.

A continental breakfast (coffee with hot milk, rolls, butter, jelly).
Un café complet.
uп ka-fay kohп-play.

For a choice of breakfast foods see page 39.

I would like . . .	. . . some ice.
Je voudrais . . .	. . . de la glace.
zhuh voo-dray . . .	. . . *duh la glahss.*

---

1. *Pronounce* ŭ *like ee with your lips in a tight circle.*
2. *zh is like the s in measure.*
3. *п means a nasal "n," pronounced through the nose.*

. . . a bottle of mineral water.
. . . une bouteille d'eau minérale.
. . . *ûne boo-tay doh mee-nay-rahl.*

Will you send these letters?	Will you put stamps on them?
Voulez-vous expédier ces lettres?	Voulez-vous les timbrer?
voo-lay-voo ex-paid-yay say lettr'?	*voo-lay-voo lay tan-bray?*

The key, please.	Is there any mail for me?
La clé, s'il vous plaît.	Y a-t-il du courrier pour moi?
la klay, seel voo play.	*ee ya teel du koor-yay poor mwà?*

Send my mail to this address.
Faites suivre mon courrier à cette adresse.
fett sweevr' mohn koor-yay ah set ah-dress.

I want to talk with the manager.
Je veux parler avec le directeur.
zhuh vuh par-lay ah-vek luh dee-rek-turr.

I need an interpreter.
J'ai besoin d'un interprète.
zhay buh-zwen dun nen-tair-pret.

Are you the chambermaid?
Etes-vous la femme de chambre?
et-voo la fahm duh shahnbr'?

Will you change the sheets?	I need . . .
Voulez-vous changer les draps?	J'ai besoin . . .
voo-lay-voo shahn-zhay lay drahp?	*zhay buh-zwen . . .*

. . . a blanket.	. . . A pillow.
. . . d'une couverture.	. . . d'un oreiller.
. . . dûne koo-vair-tûr.	*. . . dun noh-ray-yay.*

... a towel.
... d'une serviette.
... *dûne sair-v'yet.*

... some soap.
... de savon.
... *duh sa-vohn.*

... some toilet paper.
... de papier hygiénique.
... *duh pap-yay eezh-yay-neek.*

This is to be cleaned.
Ceci est à nettoyer.
suh-see ay ta net-twa-yay.

This is to be pressed.
Ceci est à repasser.
suh-see ay ta ruh-pa-say.

This is to be repaired.
Ceci est à réparer.
suh-see ay ta ray-pa-ray.

This is to be washed.
Ceci est à laver.
suh-see ay ta la-vay.

For this evening? ... tomorrow? ... tomorrow afternoon?
Pour ce soir?   ... demain? ... demain après-midi?
poor suh swahr? ... *duh-men?* ... *duh-men*
                                          ah-pray-mee-dee?

... **tomorrow evening?**
... demain soir?
... *duh-men swahr?*

When?
Quand?
kahn?

Without fail?
Sans faute?
sahn foht?

Be very careful with this.
Attention à ceci.
ah-tahns-yohn ah suh-see.

Don't press this with a hot iron.
Ne repassez pas avec un fer chaud.
nuh ruh-pa-say pa za-vek un fair shoh.

---

1. *Pronounce* û *like* ee *with your lips in a tight circle.*
2. *zh is like the s in measure.*
3. *n means a nasal "n," pronounced through the nose.*

Are my clothes ready?
Mes vêtements sont-ils prêts?
may vet-mahn sohn-teel pray?

Prepare my bill, please.
Préparez la note, s'il vous plaît.
pray-pa-ray la noht, seel voo play.

I'm leaving tomorrow morning.
Je pars demain matin.
zhuh par duh-men ma-ten.

It's very important.
C'est très important.
say tray zen-por-tahn.

Will you call me at 7 o'clock?
Voulez-vous m'appeler à sept heures?
voo-lay-voo map-lay ah set urr?

En passant: Hotel floors are generally counted starting above the ground floor—rez de chaussée—so that the second floor is called the first, the third is the second, etc.

Tips are included in the bill, but when something is brought to your room, a small tip is seldom refused.

You never have to ask for a shoeshine. Just leave your shoes outside the door when you retire. Not a bad idea, n'est-ce pas?

Point to the Answer

Veuillez indiquer ci-dessus la réponse à ma question. Merci.
Please point below to the answer to my question. Thank you.

Aujourd'hui. **Ce soir.** **Demain.** **De bonne heure.**
Today. This evening. Tomorrow. Early.

Tard. **Avant une heure.**
Late. Before one o'clock.

Avant deux (trois, quatre, cinq) heures.
Before two (three, four, five) o'clock.

A cinq (six, sept, huit, neuf, dix, onze, douze) heures.
At five (six, seven, eight, nine, ten, eleven, twelve) o'clock.

lundi	**mardi**	**mercredi**
Monday	Tuesday	Wednesday

jeudi	**vendredi**	**samedi**	**dimanche**
Thursday	Friday	Saturday	Sunday

❧ 6. Time: Hours—Days— Months

In the hotel section you noted that when making an appointment at a certain hour you simply put *à* in front of the number, and then the word for "hour." "At nine o'clock" is **à neuf heures.** The following section shows you how to tell time in greater detail, including dates. You can make all sorts of arrangements with people by indicating the hour, the day, the date, and adding the phrase **C'est entendu?** "Is it agreed?"

What time is it?	**It is one o'clock.**
Quelle heure est-il?	Il est une heure.
kell urr ay-teel?	*eel ay tŭne urr.*
It is six o'clock.	**half past . . .**
Il est six heures.	. . . et demie
eel ay see zurr.	. . . *ay duh-mee*
a quarter past . . .	**a quarter to . . .**
. . . et quart	. . . moins le quart
. . . *ay kar*	. . . *mweʀ luh kar*
ten minutes past . . .	**ten minutes to . . .**
. . . dix	. . . moins dix
. . . *deess*	. . . *mweʀ deess*
at nine o'clock	**at exactly seven o'clock**
à neuf heures	a sept heures précises
a nuff urr	*ah set urr prayseez*

---

1. *Pronounce* ŭ *like* ee *with your lips in a tight circle.*
2. *zh* is like the *s* in measure.
3. ʀ means a nasal "n," pronounced through the nose.

the morning	noon	the afternoon
le matin	midi	l'après-midi
luh ma-ten	*mee-dee*	*la-pray-mee-dee*

the evening	the night	midnight
le soir	la nuit	minuit
luh swahr	*la nwee*	*mee-nwee*

today	tomorrow	yesterday
aujourd'hui	demain	hier
oh-zhoor-dwee	*duh-men*	*ee-air*

this evening	tomorrow evening	yesterday evening
ce soir	demain soir	hier soir
suh swahr	*duh-men swahr*	*ee-air swahr*

this week	last week	next week
cette semaine	la semaine	la semaine
set suh-men	dernière	prochaine
	la suh-men	*la suh-men*
	dairn-yair	*pro-shen*

two weeks ago	this month	next month
il y a deux	ce mois-ci	le mois prochain
semaines	*suh mwa-see*	*luh mwa pro-shen*
eel ee ya duh		
suh-men		

several months ago	this year
il y a quelques mois	cette année
eel ee ya kel-kuh mwa	*set ah-nay*

last year	next year
l'année dernière	l'année prochaine
la-nay dairn-yair	*la-nay pro-shen*

five years ago
il y a cinq ans
eel ee ya seⁿ kahⁿ

1970
mille neuf cent soixante-dix
meel nuhf sahⁿ swa-sahⁿt-deess

Monday
lundi
luⁿ-dee

Tuesday
mardi
mar-dee

Wednesday
mercredi
mair-kruh-dee

Thursday
jeudi
zhuh-dee

Friday
vendredi
vahⁿ-druh-dee ·

Saturday
samedi
sam-dee

Sunday
dimanche
dee-mahⁿsh

next Monday
lundi prochain
luⁿ-dee pro-sheⁿ

last Tuesday
mardi dernier
mar-dee dairn-yay

on Fridays
le vendredi
luh vahⁿ-druh-dee

January
janvier
zhahⁿ-v'yay

February
février
fay-vree-ay

March
mars
marss

April
avril
ahv-reel

May
mai
may

June
juin
zhweⁿ

July
juillet
zhwee-yay

August
août
oo

September
septembre
sep-tahⁿbr'

---

1. *Pronounce* ũ *like* ee *with your lips in a tight circle.*
2. *zh* is like the *s* in measure.
3. ⁿ means a nasal "n," pronounced through the nose.

October	**November**	**December**
octobre	novembre	décembre
ok-tobr'	*no-vahnbr'*	*day-sahnbr'*

On what date?
À quelle date?
ah kel daht?

March 1st
Le premier mars
luh pruhm-yay marss

March 2nd, 3rd, 4th, etc.
le deux mars, le trois, le quatre
luh duh marss, luh trwa, luh katr'

The 25th of December
Le 25 décembre
luh vent-senk day-sahnbr'

Merry Christmas!
Joyeux Noël!
zhwa-yuh no-elll

The first of January
Le premier janvier
luh pruhm-yay zhahn-v'yay

Happy New Year!
Bonne Année!
bunn ah-nay!

The 14th of July
(Bastille Day)
Le quatorze juillet
luh ka-torz zhwee-yay

Long live France!
Vive la France!
veev la frahnss!

En passant: The last phrase of this section refers to Bastille Day—le Jour de la Bastille. Another occasion when everyone stops work takes place during August, when most people take an annual vacation. Shops bear the sign Fermeture Annuelle (annual closing).

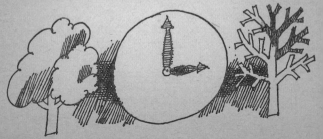

⚜ 7. French Money

This short section contains necessary vocabulary for changing money. À propos (in this regard)—you can quickly identify the French bills for 5, 10, 20, and 50 francs by their color or by the figures of French history portrayed on them.

Where can one change money?
Où peut-on changer de l'argent?
oo puh tohn shahn-zhay duh lar-zhahn?

Can I change dollars here?
Puis-je changer des dollars ici?
pweezh shahn-zhay day doh-lar ee-see?

Where is a bank?
Où y a-t-il une banque?
oo ee-ya-teel ûne bahnk?

What time does the bank open?
A quelle heure ouvre la banque?
ah kel urr oovr' la bahnk?

What time does it close?
A quelle heure ferme-t-elle?
ah kel urr fairm-tell?

What's the dollar rate?
Quel est le cours du dollar?
kel ay luh coor dû doh-lar?

It's four francs ninety to a dollar.
C'est quatre francs quatre-vingt-dix pour un dollar.
say katr' frahn katr'-ven-deess poor un doh-lar.

I would like to change $50.
Je voudrais changer cinquante dollars.
zhuh voo-dray shahn-zhay sen-kahnt doh-lar.

---

1. *Pronounce* û *like* ee *with your lips in a tight circle.*
2. zh *is like the* s *in measure.*
3. n *means a nasal "n," pronounced through the nose.*

Do you accept travelers' checks?
Acceptez-vous des chèques de voyage?
ahk-sep-tay-voo day shek duh vwa-yahzh?

Certainly.
Certainement.
sair-ten-mahn.

No, not here.
Non, pas ici.
nohn, pa zee-see.

I am sorry.
Je regrette.
zhuh ruh-grett.

Will you accept a check?
Acceptez-vous un chèque?
ahk-sep-tay-vooz un shek?

Have you any identification?
Avez-vous des papiers d'identité?
ah-vay-voo day pap-yay dee-dahn-tee-tay?

Yes, here is my passport.
Oui, voilà mon passeport.
wee, vwa-la mohn pass-por.

Give me two 100-franc notes.
Donnez-moi deux billets de cent francs.
don-nay-mwa duh bee-yay duh sahn frahn.

. . . twenty 10-franc notes.
. . . vingt billets de dix francs.
. . . ven bee-yay duh dee frahn.

I need some small change.
J'ai besoin de petite monnaie.
zhay buh-zwen duh puh-teet moh-nay.

En passant: A useful coin for tipping purposes is the 1-franc piece, worth about 20 cents.

⚜ 8. Basic Foods

The foods and drinks mentioned in this section will enable you to be well fed, and in France that is very well indeed! The section that follows this will deal with special French dishes—representative of the cuisine ("style of cooking" or "kitchen") that is one of the many outstanding products of French culture.

Breakfast
Le petit déjeûner
luh puh-tee
day-zhuh-nay

orange juice
du jus d'orange
dù zhù do-rahʀzh

a grapefruit
un pample-
mousse
uʀ pahʀ-pluh-
mooss

a continental breakfast (coffee with rolls, butter, and jam)
un café complet
uʀ ka-fay kohʀ-play.

soft boiled eggs
des oeufs à la coque
day zuh ah la kok

some toast
des toasts
day toast

fried eggs
des oeufs sur le plat.
day zuh sùr luh pla

with bacon
au bacon
oh ba-kohʀ

with ham
au jambon
oh zhahʀ-bohʀ

an omelet
une omelette
ùne om-let

scrambled eggs
des oeufs brouillés
day zuh broo-yay

coffee with hot milk
du café au lait
dù ka-fay oh lay

cocoa
du chocolat
dù sho-ko-la

tea
du thé
dù tay

---

1. *Pronounce ù like ee with your lips in a tight circle.*
2. *zh is like the s in measure.*
3. *ʀ means a nasal "n," pronounced through the nose.*

lunch
le déjeûner
luh day-zhuh-nay

dinner
le dîner
luh dee-nay

Do you know a good restaurant?
Connaissez-vous un bon restaurant?
ko-nay-say-voo un bohn ress-toh-rahn?

A table for three.
Une table pour trois.
üne tabl' poor trwa.

This way, please.
Par ici, s'il vous plaît.
par ee-see, seel voo play.

The menu, please.
La carte, s'il vous plaît.
la kart, seel voo play.

What's good?
Qu'est-ce qu'il y a de bon?
kess keel ya duh bohn?

What do you recommend?
Qu'est-ce que vous recommandez?
kess-kuh voo ruh-ko-mahn-day?

What is it?
Qu'est-ce que c'est?
kess-kuh say?

Good.
Bon.
bohn.

I'll take it.
Je le prends.
zhuh luh prahn.

First a cocktail.
D'abord un cocktail.
da-bor un kok-tail.

Then some appetizers.
Ensuite des hors d'oeuvres.
ahn-sweet day or duhvr'.

soup
du potage
dü po-tazh

fish
du poisson
dü pwa-sohn

oysters
des huitres
day zweetr'

shrimps
des.crevettes
day kruh-vet

lobster
du homard
dü oh-mar

chicken
du poulet
dù poo-lay

duck
du canard
dù ka-nahr

goose
de l'oie
duh lwah

lamb chops
des cotelettes d'agneau
day koht-let da-n'yo

roast leg of lamb
du gigot d'agneau
dù zhee-go da-n'yo

veal
du veau
dù vo

pork
du porc
dù por

roast beef
du rosbif
dù rohz-beef

hamburger
du steak haché·
dù steak ah-shay

a steak
un·steak
un steak

well done
bien cuit
b'yen kwee

medium
à point
ah pwen

rare
saignant
sen-yahn

very rare
bleu
bluh

roasted
rôti
ro-tee

broiled
grillé
gree-yay

fried
frit
free

boiled
bouilli
boo-yee

vegetables
des légumes
day lay-gùme

potatoes
des pommes de terre
day pom duh tair

fried potatoes
des pommes frites
day pom freet

rice
du ris
dù ree

noodles
des nouilles
day nwee

green beans
des haricots verts
day ar-ree-ko vair

---

1. *Pronounce* ù *like* ee *with your lips in a tight circle.*
2. zh *is like the* s *in measure.*
3. n *means a nasal "n," pronounced through the nose.*

peas
des pètits pois
day puh-tee pwa

carrots
des carottes
day ka-rot

spinach
des épinards
day zay-pee-nar

cabbage
des choux
day shoo

mushrooms
des champignons
day shahn-peen-yohn

celery
du céleri
dů sail-ree

asparagus
des asperges
day zas-pairzh

onions
des oignons
day zo-n'yohn

oil
de l'huile
duh lweel

vinegar
du vinaigre
dů vee-naigr'

salt
du sel
dů sel

lettuce
de la laitue
duh la lay-tů

tomatoes
des tomates
day to-maht

a salad
une salade
ůne sa-lahd

pepper
du poivre
dů pwavr'

mustard
de la moutarde
duh la moo-tard

with garlic
avec de l'ail
ah-vek duh l'eye

without garlic
sans ail
sahnz eye

bread
du pain
dů pan

butter
du beurre
dů burr

What wine do you recommend?
Quel vin recommandez-vous?
kel ven ruh-koh-mahn-day-voo?

white wine
du vin blanc
dů ven blahn

red wine
du vin rouge
dů ven roozh

beer
de la bière
duh la b'yair

champagne
du champagne
dŭ shahn-pine

To your health!
À votre santé!
ah votr' sahn-tay

fruits
des fruits
day frwee

grapes
des raisins
day ray-zen

peaches
des pêches
day pesh

oranges
des oranges
day zo-rahnzh

plums
des prunes
day prŭn

pears
des poires
day pwar

apples
des pommes
day pom

bananas
des bananes
day ba-nahn

a dessert
un dessert
un day-sair

pastry
de la patisserie
duh la pa-teess-ree

cake
du gateau
dŭ ga-toh

cheese
du fromage
dŭ fro-mazh

ice cream
une glace
ŭne glahss

coffee
du café
dŭ ka-fay

demi-tasse
du café noir
dŭ ka-fay nwar

expresso
café filtre
ka-fay feeltr'

tea with lemon
du thé au citron
dŭ tay oh see-trohn

hot chocolate
du chocolat
dŭ sho-ko-la

More, please.
Encore, s'il vous plaît.
ahn-kor, seel voo play.

That's enough, thank you.
C'est assez, merci.
say ta-say, mair-see.

---

1. *Pronounce ŭ like ee with your lips in a tight circle.*
2. *zh is like the s in measure.*
3. *n means a nasal "n," pronounced through the nose.*

Waiter!
Garçon!
Gar-sohn!

Waitress!
Mademoiselle!
mahd-mwa-zell!

The check, please.
L'addition, s'il vous plaît.
la-deess-yohn, seel voo play.

Is the tip included?
Service compris?
sair-veess kohn-pree?

I think there is an error in the bill.
Je crois qu'il y a une erreur dans l'addition.
zhuh krwa keel ee ya ûne air-ruhr dahn la-deess-yohn.

Oh no, sir, look here.
Oh non, monsieur, regardez.
oh nohn, muss-yuh, ruh-gar-day.

It's true.
C'est vrai.
say vray.

It's OK.
Ça va.
sa va.

Here.
Voilà.
vwa-la.

Thank you, sir.
Merci, monsieur.
mair-see, muss-yuh.

Goodbye.
Au revoir.
oh ruh-vwahr.

En passant: The reason that we have prefaced foodstuffs with du, de la, de l' and des (all variants of "some" according to the gender or number of the word) is that in French you cannot say the item by itself. Wine, for example, must always be "the wine"—le vin—or "some wine"—du vin.

Point to the Answer

Veuillez indiquer ci-dessus la réponse à ma question. Merci.
Please point below to the answer to my question. Thank
  you.

C'est la spécialité de la maison.
It's the specialty of the house.

Ça vient tout de suite.
It's ready.

Ça prendra un quart d'heure.
It takes a quarter of an hour.

Nous n'en avons pas aujourd'hui.
We don't have it today.

C'est le plat du vendredi.
That is served only on Fridays.

C'est du poulet, du porc, de l'agneau, du veau, du boeuf, du steak, du poisson, des crustacés.
It is chicken, pork, lamb, veal, beef, steak, fish, seafood.

. . . avec des légumes.   **. . . avec une sauce.**
. . . with vegetables.   . . . with a sauce.

. . . garni.
. . . with trimmings.

⚜ 9. Food Specialties of France

These expressions and names of dishes will be useful in restaurants or private homes where you may be invited. These dishes commonly appear on most French menus and are so much a part of the French dining tradition that you should recognize them on sight and know how to pronounce them as well as to enjoy them! We have written the French first, since that's how you will see it on the menu.

What is today's special?
Quelle est le plat du jour?
kel ay luh pla-du-zhoor?

Is it ready?
Est-ce que c'est prêt?
ess-kuh say pray?

How long will it take?
Combien de temps faut-il attendre?
kohn-b'yen duh tahn fo-teel ah-tahndr'?

(une) Soupe à l'oignon	(des) Escargots de Bourgogne	(des) Cuisses de Grenouille
ûne soop ah lo-n'yohn	*(day) zess-kar-go duh boor-go'yn*	*(day) kweess duh gruh-nwee*
Onion soup	Snails with garlic	Frog legs

(la) Bouillabaisse
(la) boo-ya-bayss
Fish and shellfish stew

(la) Sole aux Amandes
(la) sol oh za-maknd
Fillet of sole with almonds

(le) Vol au Vent
luh vol oh vahn
Creamed chicken, sweetbreads, and mushrooms in a pastry shell

---

1. *Pronounce* û *like* ee *with your lips in a tight circle.*
2. *zh is like the* s *in measure.*
3. *n means a nasal "n," pronounced through the nose.*

une Poule au pot
ŭne pool. oh po
Boiled chicken and
  vegetables

un Pot-au-feu
uɴ po-toh-fuh
Boiled beef and vegetables

(le) Boeuf Bourguignon
(luh) buhf boo-gheen-yohn
Beef stew with wine

(la) Quiche Lorraine
(la) keesh lo-rain
Omelet pie with ham

(le) Ris de Veau Financière
(luh) ree duh vo fee-nahɴs-yair
Sweetbreads with rich sauce

(la) Cervelle de Veau
(la) sair-vel duh vo
Calf's brains

(le) Canard à l'Orange
(luh) ka-nar ah lo-rahɴzh
Roast duck with orange sauce

(les) Tripes à la mode de
  Caen
*(lay) treep ah la mod duh
  kahɴ*
Tripe with tomatoes and
  onions

(la) Tête de Veau Vinai-
  grette
*(la) tait duh vo vee-nay-
  grett*
Calf's head with vinegar
  sauce

(une) Omelette Fines Herbes
(ŭne) om-let feen-zairb
Omelet with chopped herbs

(la) Salade Niçoise
(la) sa-lahd nee-swaz
Lettuce, tomatoes, eggs,
  anchovies etc.

(les) Coquilles St. Jacques
(lay) ko-kee seɴ zhahk
Scallops and mushrooms in
  cream sauce

(la) Blanquette de Veau
(la) blahn-kett duh vo
Veal with white wine sauce

(la) Tarte Alsacienne
(la) tart al-zass-yenn
Apple pie with custard

(les) Crêpes Suzette
(lay) krep sŭ-zett
Pancakes with orange and
  liqueur sauce

How do you like it?
Comment le trouvez-vous?
ko-mahн luh troo-vay-voo?

It's delicious!
C'est délicieux!
say day-leess-yuh!

It's exquisite!
C'est exquis!
say tex-kee!

You have an excellent chef!
Vous avez un excellent chef!
Voo za-vay uн nek-sel-lahн sheff!

What an excellent cook!
Quelle excellente cuisinière!
kel ek-sell-lahнt kwee-zeen-yair!

It was a great pleasure!
Comme c'était agréable!
kom say-tay ta-gray-ahbl'!

Thank you for a wonderful dinner!
Merci pour un dîner merveilleux!
mair-see poor uн dee-nay mair-vay-yuh.

Don't mention it, sir.
Je vous en prie, monsieur.
zhuh voo zahн pree, muss-yuh.

En passant: The phrase **je vous en prie** is a typical French expression with various meanings, among which are "I beg you," "You first," "Think nothing of it," or "Please take. this," depending on how it is used.

When you are offered something more and you say **Merci**—"Thank you"—it can mean "No, thanks." So if you do so want to accept another helping, say "A little more, thank you"—**Encore un peu, merci** (*Ahн-kor uн puh*, *mair-see*).

---

1. *Pronounce* û *like* ee *with your lips in a tight circle.*
2. *zh is like the s in measure.*
3. *н means a nasal "n," pronounced through the nose.*

⚜ 10. Transportation

Getting around by public transportation is enjoyable not only for the new and interesting things you see, but also because of the opportunities you have for practicing French. To make your travels easier, use short phrases when speaking to drivers or others when you ask directions. And don't forget **Pardon, S'il vous plaît,** and **Merci.**

Bus

The bus
L'autobus
lo-toh-bůs

Where is the bus stop?
Où est l'arrêt d'autobus?
oo ay la-ray doh-toh-bůs?

Do you go to the Rue de la Paix?
Allez-vous à la Rue de la Paix?
ah-lay voo za la rů duh la pay?

No; take number nine.
Non; prenez le numéro neuf.
nohн; pruh-nay luh nů-may-ro nuff.

How much is the fare?
C'est combien?
say kohн-b'yeн?

Where do you want to go?
Où allez-vous?
oo ah-lay voo?

To the Place Vendôme.
Place Vendôme.
plass vahн-dom.

Is it far?
C'est loin?
say lweн?

It's not far.
Ce n'est pas loin.
suh nay pa lweн.

Will you tell me where to get off?
Voulez-vous me dire où je dois descendre?
voo-lay voo muh deer oo zhuh dwa day-sahнdr'?

---

1. Pronounce *ů* like *ee* with your lips in a tight circle.
2. *zh* is like the *s* in measure.
3. *н* means a nasal "n," pronounced through the nose.

Get off here.
Descendez ici.
day-sahn-day ee-see.

En passant: You take a priority number from the bus stop
post before you get on the bus. It saves discussion of who
gets on first.

Point to the Answer

Veuillez indiquer ci-dessus la réponse à ma question. Merci.
Please point below to the answer to my question. Thank
you.

Là-bas.   **De ce côté-ci.**   **De ce côté-la.**
Over there.   This way.   That way.

De l'autre côté de la rue.   **Au coin.**
On the other side of the street.   At the corner.

À droite.   **À gauche.**   **Tout droit.**
To the right.   To the left.   Straight ahead.

Je ne sais pas.
I don't know.

Taxi

Taxi!   **Are you free?**
Taxi!   Etes-vous libre?
tak-see!   *ett-voo leebr'?*

Where to?   **To this address.**
Où allons-nous?   À cette adresse.
oo ah-lohn noo?   *ah set ah-dress.*

Do you know where it is?
Savez-vous où ça se trouve?
sa-vay-voo oo sa suh troov?

Faster, please.	**I am in a hurry.**	**Slow down.**
Plus vite, s'il vous plaît.	Je suis pressé.	Ralentissez.
Plù veet, seel voo play.	*zhuh swee pray-say.*	*Ra-lahn-tee-say.*

Stop here.	**At the corner.**
Arrêtez ici.	Au coin.
ah-ray-tay ee-see.	*oh kwen.*

Wait for me, please.	**I can't park here.**
Attendez-moi, s'il vous plaît.	Je ne peux pas stationner ici.
ah-tahn-day-mwa, seel voo play.	*zhuh nuh puh pa sta-s'yo-nay ee-see.*

I'll be back soon.	**In five minutes.**
Je reviens tout de suite.	Dans cinq minutes.
zhuh ruhv-yen tood sweet.	*dahn sen mee-nùt.*

OK. I'll wait.
Entendu. Je vous attends.
ahn-tahn-dù zhuh voo za-tahn.

How much is it by the hour?	**. . . per kilometer**
C'est combien de l'heure?	. . . du kilomètre?
say kohn-b'yen duh lurr?	*. . . dù kee-lo-metr?*

Call for me tomorrow.
Venez me chercher demain.
vuh-nay muh shair-shay duh-men.

---

1. *Pronounce ù like ee with your lips in a tight circle.*
2. *zh is like the s in measure.*
3. *n means a nasal "n," pronounced through the nose.*

Morning.	**Afternoon.**
Le matin.	L'après-midi.
luh ma-teɴ.	*la pray-mee-dee.*

At ——— o'clock.	**At the hotel ———.**
À ——— heures.	À l'hôtel ———.
ah ——— urr.	*ah lo-tel ———.*

En passant: Tip 10% or 15% of the meter. After midnight there is a surcharge on the regular fare.

Point to the Answer

Veuillez indiquer ci-dessus la réponse à ma question. Merci.
Please point below to the answer to my question. Thank you.

Je vous attendrai ici.	**Je ne peux pas attendre.**
I will wait for you here.	I can't wait.

Je reviendrai vous prendre.
I'll be back to pick you up.

Ce n'est pas assez.	**Les bagages sont en plus.**
It is not enough.	The baggage is extra.

Subway

The subway	**One first class.**	**Second class.**
Le métro	Une première.	Deuxième classe.
luh may-tro	*ůne pruhm-yair.*	*duhz'yem klahss.*

Is it direct?	**Must I change trains?**
C'est direct?	Faut-il changer?
say dee-rekt?	*foh-teel shahɴ-zhay?*

Take the line (literally, the "direction") to the Porte d'Italie.
Prenez la direction Porte d'Italie.
pruh-nay la dee-reks-yohɴ port dee-ta-lee.

Change at Châtelet.
Changez au Châtelet.
shahɴ-zhay oh shat-lay.

Then take the "direction" ———.
Puis prenez la direction ———.
pwee pruh-nay la dee-reks-yohɴ ———.

Get off at ———.
Descendez à ———.
day-sahɴ-day za ———.

I took the wrong line.
Je me suis trompé de ligne.
zhuh muh swee trohɴ-pay duh leen.

Can you help me?   **I want to go to ———.**
Pouvez vous m'aider?   Je veux aller ———.
poo-vay-voo may-day?   *zhuh vuh za-lay ———.*

En passant: Lines are all separate and are called by the name of the stop where they *end*. You can change from one to the other at the points where they intersect, called **correspondances.** Each line has a map of its stops within the car, and each station has an understandable map of the whole subway system.

---

1. *Pronounce ǔ* like *ee* with your lips in a tight circle.
2. *zh* is like the *s* in measure.
3. *ɴ* means a nasal "n," pronounced through the nose.

Train

Railroad
Chemin de fer
shuh-men duh fair

Where is the station?
Où est la gare?
oo ay la gahr?

Where does one buy tickets?
Où achète-t-on les billets?
oo a-shett-tohn lay bee-yay?

A ticket to Nice.
Un billet pour Nice.
un bee-yay poor neess.

One way only.
Aller seulement.
ah-lay suhl-mahn.

Round trip.
Aller retour.
ah-lay ruh-toor.

First class.
Première classe.
pruhm-yair klahss.

Second class.
Deuxième classe.
duhz-yehm klahss.

A timetable.
Un indicateur.
un nen-dee-ka-turr.

Where is the train to ———?
Où est le train pour ———?
oo ay luh tren poor ———?

When do we leave?
Quand partons-nous?
kahn pahr-tohn-noo?

What track?
Quelle voie?
kel vwai

Is this seat taken?
Est-ce que cette place est prise?
ess-kuh set plahss ay preez?

Will you allow me, madam?
Vous permettez, madame?
voo pair-may-tay, ma-dahm?

Go right ahead, sir.
Je vous en prie, monsieur.
zhuh voo zahn pree, muss-yuh.

What time do we get to Marseilles?
À quelle heure arrivons-nous à Marseille?
ah kel urr ah-ree-vohn noo za mar-say?

Do we stop in Tours?
On s'arrête à Tours?
ohn sa-rett ah toor?

How long are we stopping here?
Combien de temps s'arrête-t-on ici?
kohn-b'yen duh tahn sa-rett-tohn ee-see?

Where is the dining car?
Où est le wagon restaurant?
ou ay luh va-gohn ress-toh-rahn?

I can't find my ticket.
Je ne trouve pas mon billet.
zhuh nuh troov pa mohn bee-yay.

Wait! Here it is.
Attendez! Le voici.
ah-tahn-day! luh vwa-see.

Please prepare my berth.
Préparez ma couchette, s'il vous plaît.
pray-pa-ray ma koo-shett, seel voo play.

En passant: Railroads, like the subways, have First and Second Class— **Première** and **Deuxième.** When the train goes across the border to Belgium, Germany, Spain, etc., customs and passport inspection takes place on the train.

---

1. *Pronounce* ŭ *like* ee *with your lips in a tight circle.*
2. *zh is like the s in measure.*
3. *n means a nasal "n," pronounced through the nose.*

Point to the Answer

Veuillez indiquer ci-dessus la réponse à ma question. Merci.
Please point below to the answer to my question. Thank
you.

Le quai numéro ———.   **En bàs.**   **En haut.**
Track number ———.   'Downstairs.   Upstairs.

Ce' n'est pas votre train.   **Celui-ci va à ———.**
This is not your train.   This one goes to ———.

Il faudra changer à ———.
You must change at ———.

Nous arrivons à ——— heures.   **De ce côté-là.**
We arrive at ——— o'clock.   That way.

Le train part dans ——— minutes.
The train leaves in ——— minutes.

Ship

The ship.
Le bateau.
luh ba-toh.

Where is my cabin?   **Which deck?**
Où est ma cabine?   Quel pont?
oo ay ma ka-been?   *kell pohn?*

Are you the steward?
Etes-vous le steward?
ett-voo luh steward?

Where is the dining salon?
Où est la salle à manger?
oo ay la sa-la mahn-zhay?

What time are meals served?
À quelle heure sert-on les repas?
ah kell urr sair-tohn lay ruh-pa?

At what time do we sail?
A quelle heure partons-nous?
ah kell urr par-tohn-noo?.

Where is the purser?
Où est le commissaire?
oo ay luh ko-mee-sair?

I want to change tables.
Je voudrais changer de table.
zhuh voo-dray shahn-zhay duh tabl'.

(In Paris): At which pier are the sightseeing boats?
A quel quai se trouvent les bateaux-mouches?
ah kel kay suh troov lay ba-toh-moosh?

---

1. *Pronounce* û *like* ee *with your lips in a tight circle.*
2. *zh is like the s in measure.*
3. *n means a nasal "n," pronounced through the nose.*

11. Trips by Car

Car Rental

The automobile.
L'automobile.
lo-toh-mo-beel.

Where can one rent a car?
Où peut-on louer une voiture?
oo puh-tohн lway ûne vwa-tûr?

. . . a motorcycle?
. . . une motocyclette?
. . . ûne mo-toh-see-klett?

. . . a bicycle?
. . . une bicyclette?
. . . ûne bee-see-klett?.

I want to rent a car.
Je voudrais louer une voiture.
zhuh voo-dray lway ûne vwa-tûr.

How much per day?
C'est combien par jour?
say kohн-b'yeн par zhoor?

How much per kilometer?
C'est combien du kilomètre?
*say kohн-b'yen dû
kee-lo-metr'?*

Is the gasoline included?
L'essence est comprise?
lay-sahнs ay kohн-preez?

Is the transmission automatic?
Est-ce que le changement de vitesse est automatique?
ess-kuh luh shahнzh-mahн duh vee-tess ay oh-toh-ma-teek?

I would like to try it out.
Je voudrais l'essayer.
zhuh voo-dray lay-say-yay.

---

1. *Pronounce* û *like* ee *with your lips in a tight circle.*
2. *zh is like the s in measure.*
3. *н means a nasal "n," pronounced through the nose.*

En passant: Distances, except in French-speaking Canada, are reckoned in kilometers—approximately ⅝ of a mile.

Gas Station

Where can one buy gasoline?
Où peut-on acheter de l'essence?
oo puh-tohn ahsh-tay duh lay-sahns?

How much per liter? C'est combien le litre? *say kohn-b'yen luh leetr'?*	**Ten francs worth of high test.** Dix francs de super. *dee frahn duh sŭ-pair.*
Thirty liters, please. Trente litres, s'il vous plaît. *trahnt leetr', seel voo play.*	**Fill it up.** Faites le plein. *fett luh plen.*
Please— S'il vous plaît— *seel voo play—*	**Put air in the tires.** Gonflez les pneus. *gohn-flay lay p'nuh.*

Check . . . Vérifiez . . . *vay-reef-yay . . .*	**. . . the water.** . . . l'eau. *. . . lo.*	**. . . the battery.** . . . la batterie. *. . . la batt-ree.*
. . . the oil. . . . l'huile. *. . . lweel.*	**. . . the sparkplugs.** . . . les bougies. *. . . lay boo-zhee.*	**. . . the carburetor.** . . . le carburateur. *. . . luh car-bŭ-ra-turr.*
. . . the brakes. . . . les freins. *. . . lay fren.*	**Change the oil.** Changez l'huile. *shahn-zhay lweel.*	**Wash the car.** Lavez la voiture. *la-vay la vwa-tŭr.*

Grease the motor. Graissez le moteur. *gray-say luh mo-turr.*	**Change this tire.** Changez ce pneu. *shahn-zhay suh p'nuh.*

A road map, please.
Une carte routière, s'il vous plaît.
ûne kart root-yair, seel voo play.

En passant: Gas is sold by the liter (1.05 quarts). In other
words, 4 liters is about 1 gallon.

Asking Directions

Where does this road go to?
Où va ce chemin?
oo va suh shuh-men?

Is this the way to Chalons?
C'est bien la route de..Chalons?
say b'yen la root duh sha-lohn?

Is the road good?
Est-ce que la route est bonne?
ess kuh la root ay bunn?

Which is the road to Epernay?
Quelle est la route d'Épernay?
kell ay la root day-pair-nay?

It's that way. C'est par là. *say par la.*	**Is the next town far?** C'est loin la prochaine ville? *say lwen la pro-shen veel?*
Is there a good restaurant there? Y a-t-il un bon restaurant? *ee ya teel un bohn ress-toh-rahn?*	**Yes. A very good one.** Oui. Un très bon. *we. un tray bohn.*

---

1. *Pronounce û* like *ee* with your lips in a tight circle.
2. *zh* is like the *s* in measure.
3. *n* means a nasal "n," pronounced through the nose.

Is there a good hotel in Tours?
Y a-t-il un bon hôtel à Tours?
ee ya teel un bohn o-tel ah toor?

It's good enough.
C'est passable.
say pa-sahbl'.

I don't know.
Je ne sais pas.
zhuh nuh say pa.

Is it far?
C'est loin?
say lwen?

About ——— kilometers.
Environ ——— kilomètres.
ahn-vee-rohn ——— kee-lo-metr'.

Follow this road.
Suivez cette route.
swee-vay set root.

Turn right ...
Tournez à droite ...
toor-nay ah drwaht ...

as you leave the village.
en sortant du village.
ahn sohr-tahn dü vee-lazh.

When you come to the bridge ...
Quand vous arrivez au pont ...
kahn voo za-ree-vay oh pohn ...

cross it ...
traversez le ...
tra-vair-say luh ...

and turn left.
et tournez à gauche.
ay toor-nay ah gohsh.

Go straight ahead.
Allez tout droit.
ah-lay too drwa.

The road is not bad.
La route n'est pas mauvaise.
la root nay pa mo-vayz.

But ... take the expressway.
Mais ... prenez l'autoroute.
may ... pruh-nay lo-toh-root.

Point to the Answer

Veuillez indiquer ci-dessus la réponse à ma question. Merci.
Please point below to the answer to my question. Thank you.

Vous êtes ici sur la carte.
You are here on the map.

Suivez cette route-ci.
Follow this road.

La prochaine ville s'appelle ———.
The next town is called ———.

Au feu d'arrêt . . .
At the light . . .

Prenez à droite.	**Prenez à gauche.**
Turn right.	Turn left.
Allez tout droit . . .	**jusqu'à . . .**
Go straight ahead . . .	until . . .

Emergencies and Repairs

Your license!
Votre permis de conduire!
votr' pair-mee duh kohn-dweer!

---

1. *Pronounce ü* like *ee* with your lips in a tight circle.
2. *zh* is like the *s* in measure.
3. *n* means a nasal "n," pronounced through the nose.

Here it is, officer.
Le voilà, monsieur l'agent.
luh vwa-la, muss-yuh la-zhahи.

And the registration (gray card).
Et la carte grise.
ay la cart greez.

It wasn't my fault.
Ce n'était pas ma faute.
suh nay-tay pa ma foht.

The truck skidded.
Le camion a dérapé.
luh kam-yohи ah day-ra-pay.

This imbecile crashed into me.
Cet imbécile m'est rentré dedans.
set eи-bay-seel may rahи-tray duh-dahи.

En passant: As the French drive with considerable dash and challenge, **imbécile, idiot,** and **brute** are frequent and even rather mild expletives. However, control and good humor, plus a diplomatic use of French, will make driving safe and enjoyable.

I am in trouble.
Je suis en difficulté.
zhuh swee zahи dee-fee-kûl-tay.

Can you help me?
Pouvez vous m'aider?
poo-vay-voo may-day?

My car has broken down.
Ma voiture est en panne.
ma vwa-tûr ay tahи pahи.

I have a flat tire.
J'ai un pneu à plat.
zhay un p'nuh ah pla.

Can you lend me a jack?
Pouvez-vous me prêter un cric?
poo-vay-voo muh pray-tay un kreek?

Can you push me?
Pouvez vous me pousser?
poo-vay-voo muh poo-say?

Thank you very much.   You are very kind.
Merci bien.   Vous êtes très aimable.
mair-see b'yen.   *voo zett tray zay-mabl'.*

I would like to speak with the mechanic.
Je voudrais parler avec le mécanicien.
zhuh voo-dray par-lay ah-vek luh may-ka-nees-yen.

He doesn't work on the weekend.
Il ne travaille pas le weekend.
eel nuh tra-vye pa luh week-end.

The car doesn't run well.
Cette voiture ne marche pas bien.
set vwa-tur nuh marsh pa b'yen.

What is the matter?
Qu'est-ce qu'il y a?
kess-keel ee ya?

---

1. *Pronounce* ŭ *like* ee *with your lips in a tight circle.*
2. *zh is like the s in measure.*
3. *n means a nasal "n," pronounced through the nose.*

There's a noise in the motor.
Il y a un bruit dans le moteur.
eel ee ya un brwee dahn luh mo-turr.

The motor stalls.
Le moteur cale.
luh mo-turr kahl.

Difficult to start.
Difficile à démarrer.
dee-fee-seel ah day-ma-ray.

Can you fix it?
Pouvez-vous le réparer?
poo-vay-voo luh ray-pa-ray?

What will it cost?
Ce sera combien?
suh suh-ra kohn-b'yen?

How long will it take?
Combien de temps faut-il?
kohn-b'yen duh tahn fo-teel?

Today it isn't possible.
Aujourd'hui ce n'est pas possible.
oh-zhoor-dwee suh nay pa po-seebl'.

Perhaps tomorrow.
Peut-être demain.
puh-tetr' duh-men.

When will it be ready?
Quand sera-t-elle prête?
kahn suh-ra-tel prett?

In two hours.
Dans deux heures.
dahn duh zurr.

En passant: For making sure exactly when the car will be ready, consult the phrases in the "Time" section, page 33.

Some English words, like "weekend," have been adopted into French. "Cocktail," "business," "job," "cowboy," and "gangster" are other examples.

Point to the Answer

Veuillez indiquer ci-dessus la réponse à ma question. Merci.
Please point below to the answer to my question. Thank
you.

Ça va vous coûter ——— francs.
It will cost you ——— francs.

Ce sera prêt dans ——— heures.
It will be ready in ——— hours.

Ce sera prêt dans ——— jours.
It will be ready in ——— days.

Demain.   **Après-demain.**
Tomorrow.   The day after tomorrow.

Nous n'avons pas la pièce.
We don't have the part.

Nous pouvons faire une réparation provisoire.
We can make a temporary repair.

International Road Signs

DANGER

MAIN ROAD
AHEAD

SHARP TURN

CAUTION

RIGHT CURVE

LEFT CURVE

CROSSROADS

ONE WAY

**DO NOT
ENTER**

**GUARDED RR
CROSSING**

**UNGUARDED
RR CROSSING**

NO PARKING

PARKING

BUMPS

En passant: Did you notice that the bar on the international road signs mean "Stop" or "Don't"? That is why we have made use of the barred *n* as the symbol for the typical French "nasal" sound in our phonetics—to show you that you don't really pronounce the *n* but say the vowel through your nose and then cut off your breath quickly.

In addition, you will hear or see the following instructions:

Maintenez votre droite. **Ralentissez**
men-tuh-nay votr' drwaht. *ra-lahn-tee-say*
Keep to the right. Slow down

Détour **Sens unique** **Carrefour**
day-toor *sahns û-neek* *kar-foor*
Detour One way Crossroads

Vitesse maximum ——— km.
vee-tess mak-see-mum ——— kee-lo-metr'
Maximum speed ——— kilometers per hour

Serrez à gauche. **Stationnement interdit**
say-ray ah gohsh. *stass-yon-mahn an-tair-dee*
Squeeze left. No parking

Sens interdit **Interdit aux cyclistes**
sahns an-tair-dee *an-tair-dee oh see-kleest*
Do not enter No bicycle riders

piétons **Travaux**
p'yay-tohn *Tra-vo*
Pedestrians Men at work

⚜ 12. Sightseeing and Photography

We have combined these two important sections, since you will want to take pictures of what you are seeing. If you are taking pictures indoors, be sure to ask the custodian, **C'est permis?**—"Is it permitted?"

I need a guide.
J'ai besoin d'un guide.
zhay buh-zwen dun gheed.

Are you a guide?
Etes-vous guide?
ett-voo gheed?

Do you speak English?
Parlez-vous anglais?
par-lay-voo zahn-glay?

It doesn't matter.
Ça ne fait rien.
sah nuh fay r'yen.

I speak some French.
Je parle un peu français. .
zhuh parl un puh frahn-say.

How much do you charge per hour?
Combien demandez-vous de l'heure?
kohn-b'yen duh-mahn-day-voo duh lurr?

How much per day?
Combien par jour?
kohn-b'yen par zhoor?

For two people?
Pour deux personnes?
poor duh pair-sonn?

A group of four?
Un groupe de quatre?
un groop duh katr'?

Do you have a car?
Avez-vous une voiture?
ah-vay-voo zune vwa-tûr?

---

1. *Pronounce* û *like* ee *with your lips in a tight circle.*
2. *zh is like the s in measure.*
3. *n means a nasal "n." pronounced through the nose.*

We would like to see ————.
Nous voudrions voir ————.
noo voo-dree-ohn vwahr ————.

Where is the Arch of Triumph?
Où est l'Arc de Triomphe?
oo ay lark duh tree-ohnf?

Is that the Cathedral of Notre Dame?
Est-ce la cathédrale Notre-Dame?
ess la ka-tay-drahl nohtr'-dahm?

We want to go to the Louvre.
Nous voulons aller au Louvre.
noo voo-lohn za-lay oh loovr'.

To the Place de la Concorde.
Place de la Concorde.
plahss duh la kohn-kord.

To the opera.
À l'Opéra.
ah lo-pay-ra.

To the Bois Boulogne.
Au Bois de Boulogne.
oh bwah duh boo-loy'n.

To Versailles.
À Versailles.
ah vair-sye.

How beautiful!
Comme c'est beau!
kom say bo!

Very interesting.
Très intéressant.
tray zen-tay-ray-sahn.

From what period is this?
C'est de quelle époque?
say duh kell ay-pok?

Do you know a good cabaret?
Connaissez-vous un bon cabaret?
koh-nay-say-voo-zun bohn ka-ba-ray?

Let's go.
Allons-y.
ah-lohn-zee.

You are a very good guide.
Vous êtes un très bon guide.
voo zetts zun tray bohn gheed.

Come again tomorrow.
Venez encore demain.
vuh-nay zahn-kohr duh-men.

At 9 a.m.
À neuf heures du matin.
ah nuh vurr dù ma-ten.

And, if you don't have a guide:

May one enter?	**It is open.**	**It is closed.**
Peut-on entrer?	C'est ouvert.	C'est fermé.
puh-tohn nan-tray?	*say too-vair.*	*say fair-may.*

What are the visiting hours?
Quelles sont les heures de visite?
kell sohn lay zurr duh vee-zeet?

It opens at two o'clock.	**It's closed for repairs.**
Ça ouvre à deux heures.	C'est fermé pour
sa oovr' ah duh zuhr.	réparation.
	say fair-may poor
	ray-pa-ra-s'yohn.

Can one take photos?
Peut-on prendre des photos?
puh-tohn prahndr' day fo-toh?

It is permitted.	**It is forbidden.**
C'est permis.	C'est défendu.
say pair-mee.	*say day-fahn-dù.*

Check your camera.
Pas d'appareil photographique.
pa dap-pa-ray fo-toh-gra-feek.

Leave your packages in the checkroom.
Laissez les paquets au vestiaire.
lay-say lay pa-kay oh vest-yair.

---

1. *Pronounce* ù *like* ee *with your lips in a tight circle.*
2. *zh is like the s in measure.*
3. *n means a nasal "n," pronounced through the nose.*

What is the admission?
C'est combien l'entrée?
say kohn-b'yen lahn-tray?

Admission is free.
L'entrée est libre.
lahn-tray ay leebr'.

Two francs 50.
Deux francs cinquante.
duh frahn sen-kahnt.

And for children?
Et pour les enfants?
ay poor lay zahn-fahn?

Your ticket, please.
Votre billet, s'il vous plaît.
votr' bee-yay, seel voo play.

No smoking.
Défense de fumer.
day-fahnss duh fü-may.

Follow me.
Suivez-moi.
swee-vay-mwa.

This way, please.
Par ici, s'il vous plaît.
par ee-see, seel voo play.

this castle
ce château
suh sha-toh

this palace
ce palais
suh pa-lay

this church
cette église
set ay-gleez

this monument
ce monument
suh mo-nü-mahn

this street
cette rue
set rü

this square
cette place
set plahss

What is it?
Qu'est-ce que c'est?
kess kuh say?

It's magnificent!
C'est magnifique!
say mahn-yee-feek!

It is very interesting!
C'est très intéressant!
say tray zen-tay-ray-sahn!

It's very old, isn't it?
C'est très ancien, n'est-ce pas?
say tray zahnss-yen, ness-pa?

This is for you.
Voilà pour vous.
vwa-la poor voo.

Here are some signs you may see in public places and their pronunciations and meanings.

Hommes
ohm
Men

Dames
dahm
Ladies

Entrée
ahn-tray
Entrance

Sortie
sohr-tee
Exit

Ouvert
oo-vair
Open

Fermé
fair-may
Closed

Vestiaire
vess-t'yair
Checkroom

Renseignments
rahn-sayn-mahn
Information

Heures de visite
urr duh vee-zeet
Visiting hours

Tirez
tee-ray
Pull

Poussez
poo-say
Push

Chaud
sho
Hot

Froid
frwa
Cold

Défense de fumer
day-fahns duh fû-may
No smoking

Défense d'entrer
day-fahns dahn-tray
No admittance

Défense d'afficher
day-fahns da-fee-shay
No sign posting

---

1. *Pronounce û like ee with your lips in a tight circle.*
2. *zh is like the s in measure.*
3. *n means a nasal "n," pronounced through the nose.*

En passant: The term **Défense** in signs has the general connotation "no" or "Don't do it"; so when you see it, don't walk on the grass, smoke, photograph, or do whatever you might be tempted to do.

Photography

Where is a camera shop?
Où y a-t-il un magasin de photos?
oo ee-ya-teel uн ma-ga-zeн duh fo-toh?

I would like a roll of film.
Je voudrais un rouleau de pellicule.
zhuh voo-dray zuн roo-lo duh pay-lee-kŭl.

... in color.
... en couleur.
... ahн koo-lurr.

black and white.
noir et blanc.
nwahr ay blahн.

A movie film for my camera.
Un film pour ma caméra.
uн film poor ma ka-may-ra.

This is to be developed.
Ceci est à développer.
suh-see ay ta
  day-vuh-lo-pay.

How much per print?
Combien chaque photo?
kohн-b'yeн shahk fo-toh?

Two of each.
Deux de chaque.
duh duh shahk.

An enlargement.
Un aggrandissement.
uн nah-grahн-dees-mahн.

About this size.
A peu près comme ceci.
ah puh pray kom suh-see.

When will it be ready?
Quand ce sera prêt?
kahн suh-suh-ra pray?

Flash bulbs.
Des ampoules flash.
day zahн-pool flahsh.

For this camera.
Pour cet appareil.
poor set ah-pa-ray.

Can you fix this?
Pouvez-vous réparer ceci?
poo-vay-voo ray-pa-ray suh-see?

It's broken.   **May one take photos here?**
C'est cassé.   Peut-on prendre des photos ici?
say ka-say.   *puh-tohн prahнdr' day fo-toh ee-see?*

Pardon me, Miss,   **will you permit me**
Je m'excuse, Mademoiselle,   me permettez-vous
rhuh mek-skŭz, mahd-mwa-zell,   *muh pair-may-tay-voo*

to take a photo of you?   **Stand here.**
de prendre une photo de vous?   Mettez-vous là.
duh prahнdr' ŭne fo-toh duh voo?   *may-tay voo la*

Don't move.   **Smile!**   **That's it!**
Ne bougez pas.   Souriez!   C'est ça!
nuh boo-zhay pa.   *soo-ree-ay.*   *say sa.*

Will you kindly take one of me?
Voulez-vous bien en prendre une de moi?
voo-lay-voo b'yeн nahн prahнdr' ŭne duh mwa?

In front of this door.   **You are very kind.**
Devant cette porte.   Vous êtes bien aimable.
duh-vahн set port.   *voo zett b'yeн nay mahbl'.*

May I send you one?
Peut-on vous en envoyer une?
puh-tohн voo zahн nahн-vwah-yay ŭne?

Your name?   **Your address?**
Votre nom?   Votre adresse?
votr' nohн?   *votr' ah-dress?*

---

1. *Pronounce ŭ like ee with your lips in a tight circle.*
2. *zh is like the s in measure.*
3. *н means a nasal "n," pronounced through the nose.*

En passant: Asking to take pictures of someone often leads to more general conversation. For this reason the following three sections will be especially interesting to you.

Point to the Answer

Veuillez indiquer ci-dessus la réponse à ma question. Merci.
Please point below to the answer to my question. Thank you.

Revenez demain.   **À ——— heures.**
Come back tomorrow.   At ——— o'clock.

Revenez dans ——— jours.
Come back in ——— days.

Nous pouvons le réparer.
We can repair it.

Nous ne pouvons pas le réparer.
We cannot repair it.

Nous n'en avons pas.
We haven't any.

⚜·13. Entertainment

This section shows you how to extend and accept invitations and suggest things to do, and it gives some typical conversations for theaters or night clubs and some suitable words of appreciation when you are asked for dinner.

Things to Do

May I invite you . . .
Est-ce que je peux vous inviter . . .
ess kuh zhuh puh voo zen-vee-tay . . .

. . . to dinner?
. . . à dîner?
. . . ah dee-nay?

. . . to lunch?
. . . à déjeuner?
. . . ah day-zhuh-nay?

. . . to have a drink?
. . . à prendre un verre?
. . . ah prahn-dr' un vair?

. . . to dance?
. . . à danser?
. . . ah dahn-say?

. . . to go for a drive?
. . . à faire une promenade en voiture?
. . . ah fair ŭne prom-nahd ahn vwah-tŭr?

. . . to play bridge?
. . . à jouer au bridge?
. . . ah zhoo-ay oh bridge?

. . . to the movies?
. . . au cinéma?
. . . oh see-nay-ma?

. . . to the theater?
. . . au théâtre?
. . . oh tay-ahtr'?

. . . to play golf?
. . . à jouer au golf?
. . . ah zhoo-ay oh gohlf?

---

1. Pronounce *ŭ* like *ee* with your lips in a tight circle.
2. *zh* is like the *s* in measure.
3. *n* means a nasal "n," pronounced through the nose.

... to play tennis?
... à jouer au tennis?
... *ah zhoo-ay oh tay-nees?*

Thank you very much.
Merci bien.
mair-see b'yen.

With pleasure.
Avec plaisir.
ah-vek play-zeer.

I am sorry.
Je regrette.
zhuh ruh-grett.

I cannot.
Je ne peux pas.
zhuh nuh puh pa.

I am busy.
Je suis occupé.
zhuh swee zo-kü-pay.

I am waiting for someone.
J'attends quelqu'un.
zha-tahn kel-kun.

I am tired.
Je suis fatigué.
zhuh swee fa-tee-gay.

I don't feel well.
Je ne me sens pas bien.
*zhuh nuh muh sahn pa
    b'yen.*

Perhaps another time.
Peut-être une autre fois.
puh-tetr' üne oh-tr' fwa.

**Where are we going
    tomorrow?**
Où allons-nous demain?
oo ah-lohn-noo duh-men?

Let's go ...
Allons ...
ah-lohn ...

... around town.
... visiter la ville.
... vee-zee-tay la veel.

... to see a fashion show.
... voir une présentation de couture.
... vwahr üne pray-zahn-tahs-yohn duh koo-tür.

... to an art show.
... voir une exposition de peinture.
... vwahr üne ex-po-zeess-yohn duh pen-tür.

... to the film festival.
... au Festival du Film.
... oh fes-tee-vahl dü film.

... to the opera.
... à l'Opéra.
... ah lo-pay-ra.

... **to see a new play.**
... voir une nouvelle pièce.
... *vwahr ûne noo-vel p'yess.*

... **to the auto show.**
... au Salon de l'Auto.
... *oh sa-lohn duh loh-toh.*

... **to the meeting.**
... à la réunion.
... *ah la ray-ûn-yohn.*

... **to the Flea Market.**
... au Marché aux Puces.
... *oh mar-shay oh pûss*

... **to take a trip on the Seine.**
... faire une promenade sur la Seine.
... *fair ûne prom-nahd sûr la sain.*

... **to see a soccer game.**
... voir un match de football.
... *vwahr un match duh foot-ball.*

... **to the races.**
... aux courses.
... *oh koors.*

Who is ahead?
Qui mène?
kee main?

Theaters and Nightclubs

What's playing?
Qu'est-ce qu'on joue?
kess kohn zhoo?

Two seats, please.
Deux places, s'il vous plaît.
duh plahss, seel voo play.

... **in the orchestra.**
... à l'orchestre.
... *a lohr-kestr'.*

... **in the balcony.**
... au balcon.
... *oh bahl-kohn.*

Are they good seats?
Ce sont de bonnes places?
suh sohn duh bunn plahss?

---

1. *Pronounce* û *like* ee *with your lips in a tight circle.*
2. *zh is like the* s *in measure.*
3. *n means a nasal "n," pronounced through the nose.*

When does it start?
Quand commence-t-on?
kahn ko-mahnss-tohn?

What do you think of it?
Qu'est-ce que vous en pensez?
kess kuh voo zahn pahn-say?

It's very good.
C'est très bien.
say tray b'yen.

It's great!
C'est formidable!
say for-mee-dahbl'!

Who is playing the lead?
Qui joue le rôle principal?
*kee zhoo luh roll
    pren-see-pal?*

She is beautiful.
Elle est belle.
ell ay bell.

It's very amusing.
C'est très amusant.
say tray za-mù-zahn.

Is it over?
C'est fini?
say fee-nee?

Let's go to a nightclub.
Allons dans un cabaret.
ah-lohn dahn zun ka-ba-ray.

A table near the dance floor.
Une table près de la piste.
ùne tabl' pray duh la peest.

Is there a minimum charge?
Est ce qu'il y a un tarif minimum?
ess keel ee ya un ta-reef mee-nee-mum?

For the first drink, 40 francs.
Pour la première consommation quarante francs.
poor la pruhm-yair kohn-so-mahs-yon ka-rahnt frahn.

Shall we dance?
On danse?
ohn dahnss?

Shall we stay?
On reste?
ohn rest?

Let's leave.
Partons.
par-tohn.

An Invitation to Dinner

Can you come to dinner at our house?
Pouvez-vous venir dîner chez nous?
poo-vay-voo vuh-neer dee-nay shay noo?

. . . **Monday at 8?**
. . . lundi à huit heures?
. . . *luɴ-dee ah wee turr?*

With pleasure.
Avec plaisir.
ah-vek play-zeer.

If it isn't inconvenient for you.
Si ça ne vous dérange pas.
see sa nuh voo day-rahɴzh-pa.

Very happy to see you.
Très content de vous voir.
tray kohɴ-tahɴ duh voo vwahr.

Sorry I'm late.
Je regrette d'être en retard.
*zhuh ruh-gret detr' ahɴ
    ruh-tar.*

The traffic was terrible!
La circulation était terrible!
*la seer-kǔ-las'yohɴ ay-tay
    tair-reebl'!*

Make yourself at home.
Faîtes comme chez vous.
fet kom shay voo.

What a beautiful house!
Quelle belle maison!
kell bell may-zohɴ!

Will you have something to drink?
Voulez-vous boire quelque chose?
voo-lay-voo bwahr kel-kuh shohz?

A cigarette?
Une cigarette?
ǔne see-ga-rett?

To your health!
À votre santé!
ah votr' sahɴ-tay!

Dinner is served.
Le dîner est servi.
luh dee-nay ay sair-vee.

Will you sit here?
Voulez-vous vous asseoir
    ici?
*voo-lay-voo voo za-swahr
    ee-see?*

What an excellent meal!
Quel excellent repas!
kel ek-say-lahɴ ruh-pa!

---

1. *Pronounce ǔ like ee with your lips in a tight circle.*
2. *zh is like the s in measure.*
3. *ɴ means a nasal "n," pronounced through the nose.*

But have some more!
Mais reprenez-en!
may ruh-pruh-nay-zahн!

We had a wonderful time.
On s'est bien amusé.
ohн say b'yeн na-mü-zay.

One (I, we) must go.
Il faut partir.
eel fo par-teer.

What a shame
Quel dommage!
kel doh-mazh!

I'll drive you back.
Je vais vous reconduire.
zhuh vay voo ruh-kohн-dweer.

No, please don't bother.
Non, je vous en prie, ne vous dérangez pas.
nohн, zhuh voo zahн pree, nuh voo day-rahн-zhay pa.

Thank you for your great hospitality.
Merci de votre bonne hospitalité.
mair-see duh votr' bunn oss-pee-ta-lee-tay.

En passant: You can get a lot of conversational mileage out of the expression **Il faut** followed by the infinitive of the verb (the form given in the dictionary). **Il faut** by context means either "I must," "One must," or "You," "he," "she," "it," "we," or "they must." The negative **ne . . . pas** fits around it—**Il ne faut pas**—"One must not," etc.

⚜ 14. Talking to People

Phrase books are generally too preoccupied with attending to your wants and the need for "getting along" to pay much attention to what you should say when you are introduced to someone. The following expressions have been tested for everyday conversational frequency and, except for the rather special ones at the end of the section, will be of immediate use for making conversation with anyone you may meet.

Do you live in this city?
Vous habitez cette ville?
voo za-bee-tay set veel?

From what part of the country do you come?
De quelle région venez-vous?
duh kel rayzh-yohn vuh-nay-voo?

I am from Nancy.
Je suis de Nancy.
zhuh swee duh nahn-see.

Really?
Vraiment?
vray-mahn?

It's a beautiful city.
C'est une très belle ville.
say tůne tray bel veel.

---

1. *Pronounce ů* like *ee* with your lips in a tight circle.
2. *zh* is like the *s* in measure.
3. *n* means a nasal "n," pronounced through the nose.

I've been there.
J'y ai été.
zhee yay ay-tay.

I would like to go there.
J'aimerais y aller.
zhaim-ray ee ah-lay.

How long have you been here?
Depuis quand êtes-vous ici?
duh-pwee kahn et-voo zee-see?

For three days.
Depuis trois jours.
duh-pwee trwa zhoor.

Several weeks.
Quelques semaines.
kel-kuh suh-men.

Two months.
Deux mois.
duh mwa.

How long will you stay here?
Combien de temps allez-vous rester ici?
kohn-b'yen duh tahn ah-lay voo ress-tay ee-see?

I will stay ————.
Je reste ————.
zhuh rest ————.

Have you been in France before?
Avez-vous déjà été in France?
ah-vay-yoo day-zha ay-tay ahn frahnss?

No, never.
Non, jamais.
nohʀ, zha-may.

Yes, I've been here before.
Oui, j'y ai déjà été.
wee, zhee yay day-zha ay-tay.

Once.
Une fois.
ŭne fwa.

Five years ago.
Il y a cinq ans.
eel ee ya seʀk ahʀ.

Where are you living?
Où habitez-vous?
oo ah-bee-tay-voo?

At what hotel?
A quel hôtel?
ah kel o-tel?

What do you think of Paris?
Comment trouvez-vous Paris?
ko-mahʀ troo-vay-voo pa-ree?

I like it very much.
Je l'aime beaucoup.
zhuh laim bo-koo.

It is very interesting.
C'est très intéressant.
say tray zeʀ-tay-ray-sahʀ.

The city is beautiful.
La ville est belle.
la veel ay bell.

---

1. *Pronounce ŭ* like *ee* with your lips in a tight circle.
2. *zh* is like the *s* in measure.
3. *ʀ* means a nasal "n," pronounced through the nose.

The women are beautiful.
Les femmes sont belles.
lay fahm sohn bell.

Have you been in Normandy?
Avez-vous été en Normandie?
ah-vay voo zay-tay ahn nor-mahn-dee?

You must go there.
Il faut y aller.
eel fo tee ah-lay.

En passant: When someone asks whether you have visited certain sections of France, you should be able to identify these areas by their regional names, which may not appear on a map and may be quite different from the English. Among these names are:

La Côte d'Azur
la koht da-zür
The Mediterranean coast of France

La Bourgogne
la boor-goy'n
Burgundy

Le Midi
luh mee-dee
The south of France

The names of the other sections resemble their English equivalents.

Les Châteaux de la Loire
lay sha-toh duh la lwahr
The Chateaux of the Loire Valley

La Rive Gauche
la reev gohsh
The "Left Bank" (in Paris)

Are you from the United States?
Venez-vous des États-Unis?
vuh-nay-voo day zay-ta-zŭ-nee?

Yes, I am from San Francisco.
Oui, je suis de San Francisco.
wee, zhuh swee duh san francisco..

I speak French just a little.
Je parle français un tout petit peu.
zhuh parl frahn-say un too ptee puh.

But you have a good accent.
Mais vous avez un bon accent.
mais voo za-vay un bohn nakh-sahn

You are very kind.
Vous êtes très aimable.
voo zett tray zay-mabl'.

Have you been to America?
Avez-vous été en Amérique?
ah-vay voo zay-tay ahn na-may-reek?

Where have you been?
Où avez-vous été?
oo ah-vay-voo zay-tay?

---

1. *Pronounce ŭ like ee* with your lips in a tight circle.
2. *zh* is like the *s* in measure.
3. *n* means a nasal "n," pronounced through the nose.

You must come to see us.
Il faut venir nous voir.
eel fo vuh-neer noo vwahr.

At our house.
Chez nous.
shay noo.

What do you think of ———?
Que pensez-vous de ———?
kuh pahn-say-voo duh ———?

Do you like ———?
Aimez-vous ———?
ay-may voo ———?

When people ask your opinion about something, you will find the following comments most helpful:

Magnificent.
Magnifique.
mahn-yee-feek.

Wonderful.
Formidable.
for-mee-dabl'.

Very interesting.
Très intéressant.
tray zen-tay-ray-sahn.

Not bad.
Pas mal.
pa mahl

Sometimes.
Quelquefois.
kel-kuh-fwa.

Often.
Souvent.
soo-vahn.

Once.
Une fois.
ûne fwa.

Never.
Jamais.
zha-may.

It seems to me that ———.
Il me semble que ———.
eel muh sahnbl' kuh ———.

In any case . . .
En tout cas . . .
ahn too ka . . .

It's a shame!
C'est dommage!
say doh-mazh!

I don't know.
Je ne sais pas.
zhuh nuh say pa.

I have forgotten.
J'ai oublié.
zhay oo-blee-yay.

I agree with you.
Je suis d'accord.
zhuh swee da-kor.

You are right.
Vous avez raison.
voo za-vay ray-zohn.

Are you married?
Etes vous marié?
ett voo mar-yay?

I am married.
Je suis marié.
zhuh swee mar-yay.

I am not married.
Je ne suis pas marié.
zhuh nuh swee pa mar-yay.

Is your wife here?
Est-ce que votre femme est
là?
ess kuh votr' fahm ay la?

Is your husband here?
Est-ce que votre mari est
là?
ess kuh votr' ma-ree ay la?

Do you have any children?
Avez-vous des enfants?
ah-vay voo day zahn-fahn?

Yes, I have. .
Oui, j'en ai.
wee, zhahn nay.

No, I have not.
Non, je n'en ai pas.
nohn, zhuh nahn nay pa.

---

1. *Pronounce* ũ *like* ee *with your lips in a tight circle.*
2. *zh is like the s in measure.*
3. *n means a nasal "n," pronounced through the nose.*

How many boys?	How many girls?
Combien de garçons?	Combien de filles?
kohn-b'yen duh gar-sohn?	*kohn-b'yen duh fee?*

How old are they?	My son is seven years old.
Quel âge ont-ils?	Mon fils a sept ans.
kel azh ohn-teel?	*mohn fees ah set ahn.*

My daughter is ten years old.	What charming children!
Ma fille a dix ans.	Quels enfants charmants!
ma fee ya dee zahn.	*kel zahn-fahn shar-mahn!*

Is it possible?	Why not?
Est-ce possible?	Pourquoi pas?
ess po-seebl'?	*poor-kwa pa?*

This is . . .	. . . my . . .	. . . your . . .
C'est . . .	. . . ma . . .	. . . votre . . .
say . . .	*. . . ma . . .*	*. . . votr' . . .*

. . . his (or her) . . .	. . . mother.
. . . sa . . .	. . . mère.
. . . sa . . .	*. . . mair.*

. . . sister.	. . . wife.	. . . daughter.
. . . soeur.	. . . femme.	. . . fille.
. . . surr.	*. . . fahm.*	*. . . fee.*

. . . daughter-in-law.	. . . grandaughter.
. . . belle-fille.	. . . petite-fille
. . . bell-fee.	*. . . puh-teet-fee.*

This is . . .	. . . my . . .	. . . your . . .
C'est . . .	. . . mon . . .	. . . votre . . .
say . . .	*. . . mohn . . .*	*. . . votr' . . .*

... his (or her) ...   ... father.
... son ...   ... père.
... sohn ...   ... pair.

... brother.   ... husband.   ... son.
... frère.   ... mari.   ... fils.
... frair.   ... ma-ree.   ... feess.

... son-in-law.   ... grandson.
... beau-fils.   ... petit-fils.
... bo-feess.   ... puh-tee-feess.

Do you know ...   ... that man?
Connaissez-vous ...   ... cet homme?
ko-ñay-say-voo ...   ... set ohm?

He is ...   ... a writer.
C'est ...   ... un écrivain.
say ...   ... tun ay-kree-ven.

... an artist.   ... an actor.
... un artiste.   ... un acteur.
... tun nar-tees   ... tun nak-turr.

... a business   ... a lawyer.
   man.   ... un avocat.
... un homme   ... tun na-vo-ka.
   d'affaires.
... tun nohm
   da-fair.

---

1. *Pronounce* ů like *ee* with your lips in a tight circle.
2. *zh* is like the *s* in measure.
3. *n* means a nasal "n," pronounced through the nose.

... a manu-.
facturer.
... un fabricant.
... tun
fa-bree-kahn.

... a doctor.
... un médecin.
... tun maid-sen.

... a banker.
... un banquier.
... tun
bahnk-yay.

... a professor.
... un professeur.
... tun pro-fay-surr.

... a military man.
... un militaire.
... tun mee-lee-tair.

... a politician.
... un homme de politique.
... tun nohm duh
po-lee-teek.

... my husband.
... mon mari.
... mohn ma-ree.

Do you know ...
Connaissez-vous ...
ko-nay-say-voo ...

... that lady?
... cette dame?
... sett dahm?

She is ...
C'est ...
say ...

... a singer.
... une chanteuse.
... tune shahn-turs ...

... an actress.
... une actrice.
... tune ak-treess.

... my wife.
... ma femme.
... ma fahm.

Artist, writer, professor, doctor, and certain other pro-
fessions are the same for masculine and feminine.

He is American.
Il est américain.
eel ay ta-may-ree-ken.

She is American.
Elle est américaine.
el ay ta-may-ree-kain.

He is French.
Il est français.
eel ay frahn-say.

She is French.
Elle est française.
el ay frahn-sayz.

He is German.
Il est allemand.
eel ay tahl-mahн.

She is German.
Elle est allemande.
el ay tahl-mahнd.

He is English.
Il est anglais.
eel ay tahн-glay.

She is English.
Elle est anglaise.
el ay tahн-glayz.

He is Canadian.
Il est canadien.
eel ay ka-nahd-yeн.

She is Canadian.
Elle est canadienne.
el ay ka-nahd-yen.

He is Italian.
Il est italien.
eel ay tee-tal-yeн.

She is Italian.
Elle est italienne.
el ay tee-tal-yen.

Very nice.
Très sympathique.
tray seн-pa-teek.

Very intelligent.
Très intelligent. (m)
   Très intelligente. (f)
tray zeн-tay-lee-zahн.
   tray zeн-tay-lee-zhahнt.

Very pretty.
Très jolie. (f)
tray zho-lee.

Very capable.
Très capable.
tray ka-pabl'.

Here is my address.
Voici mon adresse.
vwa-see mohн na-dress.

What is your address?
Quelle est votre adresse?
kel ay votr' ah-dress?

Here is my telephone number.
Voici mon numéro de téléphone.
vwa-see mohн nŭ-may-ro duh tay-lay-fohn.

What is your telephone number?
Quel est votre numéro de téléphone?
kel ay votr' nŭ-may-ro duh tay-lay-fohn?

---

1. *Pronounce* ŭ *like* ee *with your lips in a tight circle.*
2. *zh is like the* s *in measure.*
3. *н means a nasal "n," pronounced through the nose.*

May I call you?
Est-ce que je peux vous appeler?
ess kuh zhuh puh voo zap-lay?

When?	**Tomorrow morning.**	**Early.**
Quand?	Demain matin.	De bonne heure.
kahn?	*duh-men ma-ten.*	*duh bunn urr.*

Late in the afternoon.	**Where?**
En fin d'après-midi.	Où?
ahn fen da-pray-mee-dee.	*oo?*

What is your first name?	**Mine is Richard.**
Quel est votre prénom?	Le mien, c'est Richard.
kel ay votr' pray-nohn?	*luh m'yen, say ree-shar.*

You are very pretty.	**You are very kind.**
Vous êtes très jolie.	Vous êtes bien aimable.
voo zett tray zho-lee.	*voo zett b'yen nay-mabl'.*

You dance very well.	**You sing very well.**
Vous dansez très bien.	Vous chantez très bien.
voo dahn-say tray b'yen.	*voo shahn-tay tray b'yen.*

What a pretty dress!
Quelle jolie robe!
kel zho-lee rohb!

I have a surprise for you.	**Do you like it?**
J'ai une surprise pour vous.	Ça vous plait?
zhay ŭne sŭr-preez poor voo.	*sa voo play?*

Can we see each other again?
Est-ce que nous pouvons nous revoir?
ess kuh noo poo-vohn noo ruh-vwahr?

What's the matter?
Qu'est-ce qu'il ya?
kess keel ya?

Are you angry?
Etes-vous fâché? (-e)
ett-voo fa-shay?

Why?
Pourquoi?
poor-kwa?

Where are you going?
Où allez-vous?
oo ah-lay voo?

Let's go together.
Allons-y ensemble.
ah-lohn zee ahn-sahnbl'.

You are very beautiful.
Vous êtes très belle.
voo zett tray bell.

You are very nice.
Vous êtes très sympathique.
voo zett tray sen-pa-teek.

What do you think of me?
Qu'est-ce que vous pensez de moi?
kess kuh voo pahn-say duh mwa?

I like you very much.
Vous me plaisez beaucoup.
voo muh play-zay bo-koo.

I love you.
Je vous aime. (formal)
zhuh voo zaim.
Je t'aime. (informal)
zhuh taim.

Really?
Vraiment?
vray-mahn?

No fooling?
Sans blague?
sahn blahg?

Have you a picture?
Avez-vous une photo?
ah-vay-voo zŭne fo-toh?

For me?
Pour moi?
poor mwa?

Will you write me?
Est-ce que vous m'écrirez?
ess-kuh voo may-kree-ray?

I won't forget you.
Je ne vous oublierai pas.
zhuh nuh voo zoo-blee-ray pa.

---

1. *Pronounce* ŭ *like* ee *with your lips in a tight circle.*
2. *zh is like the* s *in measure.*
3. *n means a nasal "n," pronounced through the nose.*

⚜ 15. Words That Show You Are "With It"

There are certain words constantly used by French people that do not have an exact equivalent in English. To use them at the right time will make it appear that you have not only a diploma in good manners but also an excellent foundation in French culture patterns. In other words, you are "with it."

We have divided these phrases into two groups. The first is composed of selected polite expressions:

Bravo!
bra-vo!
Good (for you)!

Bon séjour!
bohn say-zhoor!
Have a good stay!

A votre santé!
ah votr' sahn-tay!
To your health!

Mes amitiés à ———
may za-meet-yay ah ———
My regards to ———

Amusez-vous bien!
ah-mŭ-zay-voo b'yen!
Have a good time!

Félicitations.
fay-lee-see-tass-yohn.
Congratulations!

Bon voyage!
bohn vwa-yazh!
Have a good trip!

Faites comme chez vous!
fett kom shay voo!
Make yourself at home!

Mes compliments!
may kohn-plee-mahn!
My compliments!

Bon appétit!
bohn na-pay-tee!
Good appetite!

Au plaisir.
oh play-zeer.
Goodbye. (very polite)

Bonne chance!
bunn shahnss!
Good luck!

---

1. *Pronounce* ŭ *like* ee *with your lips in a tight circle.*
2. *zh is like the s in measure.*
3. *n means a nasal "n," pronounced through the nose.*

Because the following phrases occur frequently in conversation, it will interest you to know what they mean, as well as to learn to use them as conversational stopgaps. The translations are rather free, as these expressions are very idiomatic.

Je vous en prie.
zhuh voo zahn pree.
Please do so.

Ce n'est rien.
suh nay r'yen.
It's really nothing.

Allez-y!
ah-lay zee!
Go right ahead!

Donc ...
dohnk ...
Then ...

Voyons.
vwa-yohn.
Let's see.

Entendu ...
ahn-tahn-dü ...
It's understood ...

D'accord.
da-kor.
I agree. (It's agreed.)

Mon Dieu!
mohn d'yuh!
Heavens! (My God!)

Allons donc.
ah-lohn dohnk.
Well, now.

Formidable!
for-mee-dahbl'!
Just great!

N'est-ce pas?
ness pa?
Isn't it? (Isn't that right?)

Ça va?
sa va?
Is it all right?
   (How's it going?)

Ça va.
sa va.
It's all right.
   (It's going fine.)

Quand même.
kahn mem.
Well, really! (In any case.)

Eh bien ...
eh b'yen ...
Well ...

Alors ...
ah-lor ...
Then ... (and what?)

Quoi?
kwa?
What?

Ne vous en faites pas.
nuh voo zahн fett pa.
Don't worry about it.

Comment?
ko-mahн?
How's that?

Ce n'est pas la peine.
suh nay pa la pain.
It's not worth the trouble.

À la bonne heure!
ah la bunn nurr!
Fine!

Figurez-vous!
fee-gǔ-ray-voo!
Just imagine!

N'importe quoi.
neн-port kwa.
Anything at all.

Ça m'est égal.
sa may tay-gahl.
It's all the same to me.

Ça y est!
sa ee ay!
That's it!

Ne vous dérangez pas!
nuh voo day-rahн-zhay pa!
Don't bother!

⚜ 16. Shopping

Shops in France still tend to be specialized, although there exist chains of general stores and even the supermarket—supermarché.

Names of Shops

Where can one find . . .
Où peut-on trouver . . .
oo puh-tohн troo-vay . . .

. . . a dress shop?
. . . une maison de couture?
. . . *ûne may-zohн duh koo-tûr?*

. . . a shoe store?
. . . un magasin de chaussures?
. . . *uн ma-ga-zeн duh sho-sûr?*

. . . a drug store?
. . . une pharmacie?
. . . *ûne far-ma-see?*

. . . a toy shop?
. . . un magasin de jouets?
. . . *uн ma-ga-zeн duh zhoo-ay?*

. . . a flower shop?
. . . un fleùriste?
. . . *uн fluh-reest?*

. . . a department store?
. . . un grand magasin?
. . . *uн grahн ma-ga-zeн?*

. . . a hat shop?
. . . une modiste?
. . . *ûne mo-deest?*

. . . a jewelry shop?
. . . une bijouterie?
. . . *ûne bee-zhoo-tree?*

. . . a book shop?
. . . une librairie?
. . . *ûne lee-bray-ree?*

. . . an antique shop?
. . . un antiquaire?
. . . *uн нahн-tee-kair?*

---

1. *Pronounce û like ee* with your lips in a tight circle.
2. *zh* is like the *s* in measure.
3. *н* means a nasal "n," pronounced through the nose.

... **a grocery store?**
... un magasin d'alimentation?
... *un ma-ga-zen da-lee-mahn-tas-yohn?*

... **a camera shop?**
... un magasin de photographie?
... *un ma-ga-zen duh fo-toh-gra-fee?*

... **a market?**
... un marché?
... *un mar-shay?*

... **a perfume shop?**
... une parfumerie?
... *une par-fü-muh-ree?*

... **a tobacco shop?**
... un bureau de tabac?
... *un bü-ro duh ta-ba?*

... **a barber shop?**
... un coiffeur?
... *un kwa-fur?*

... **a beauty shop?**
... un salon de beauté?
... *un sa-lohn duh bo-tay?*

En passant: Although **magasin** is the usual word for "shop," **boutique** is also very much in use. On shop signs you will sometimes see the word **chez** followed by a name. **Chez Marcelle,** for example, means "At Marcelle's."

General Shopping Vocabulary

May I help you?
Puis-je vous aider?
pweezh voo zay-day?

What do you wish?
Vous désirez?
voo day-zee-ray?

I would like to buy ...
Je voudrais acheter ...
zhuh voo-dray zash-tay ...

... **a present for my husband.**
... un cadeau pour mon mari.
... *un ka-do poor mohn ma-ree.*

... **a present for my wife.**
... un cadeau pour ma femme.
... *un ka-do poor ma fahm.*

... **something for a man.**
... quelque chose pour un homme.
... *kel-kuh shozh poor un nohm.*

... **for a girl.**	... **for a lady.**
... pour une jeune fille.	... pour une dame.
... *poor ùne zhuhn fee.*	... *poor ùne dahm.*

Nothing for the moment.	**I'm just looking around.**
Rien pour le moment.	Je regarde seulement.
r'yen poor luh mo-mahn.	*zhuh ruh-gard suhl-mahn.*

I'll be back later.	**I like this.**	... **that.**
Je reviens plus tard.	J'aime ceci.	... cela.
zhuh ruh-v'yen plù tar.	*zhaim suh-see.*	... *suh-la.*

How much is it?	**Show me another.**
C'est combien?	Montrez m'en un autre.
say kohn-b'yen?	*mohn-tray mahn un notr'.*

Something less expensive.
Quelque chose de moins cher.
kel-kuh shohz duh mwen shair.

Do you like this?	**May I try it on?**
Aimez-vous cela?	Est-ce que je peux l'essayer?
ay-may-voo suh-la?	*ess kuh juh puh lay-say-yay?*

That suits you marvelously.
Ça vous va à merveille.
sa voo va ah mair-vay.

Can you alter it?
Pouvez-vous arranger cela?
poo-vay-voo zah-rahn-zhay suh-la?

---

1. *Pronounce* ù *like* ee *with your lips in a tight circle.*
2. *zh is like the s in measure.*
3. *n means a nasal "n," pronounced through the nose.*

Is it handmade?
Est-ce que c'est fait à la main?
ess kuh say fay ta la men?

... hand embroidered?
... brodé à la main?
... bro-day ah la men?

Good, I'll take it.
Bon, je·le prends.
bohn, zhuh luh prahn.

Can one pay by check?
On peux payer par chèque?
ohn puh pay-yay par shek?

The change, please.
La monnaie, s'il vous plaît.
la mo-nay, seel voo play.

A receipt, please.
Un reçu, s'il vous plaît.
un ruh-sû, seel voo play.

Will you wrap it?
Voulez-vous l'emballer?
voo-lay-voo lahn-ba-lay?

Can you send it?
Pouvez-vous l'expédier?
poo-vay-voo lex-paid-yay?

... to this address?
... à cette adresse?
... ah set ah-dress?

Come see us again!
Revenez nous voir!
ruh-vuh-nay noo vwahr!

On sale.
En solde.
ahn sold.

Bargain sale.
Solde d'occasions.
sold do-kaz-yohn.

Point to the Answer

Veuillez indiquer ci-dessus la réponse à ma question. Merci.
Please point below to the answer to my question. Thank you.

Nous n'en avons pas.
We haven't any.

Nous n'avons rien de plus grand.
We haven't anything larger.

Nous n'avons rien de plus petit.
We haven't anything smaller.

Nous ne livrons pas.
We don't deliver.

Nous pouvons l'envoyer à une adresse en Amérique.
We can send it to an address in America.

Quelle est votre adresse?
What is your address?

Nous regrettons, mais nous ne pouvons pas accepter de chèque à votre nom.
We are sorry, but we cannot accept personal checks.

Nous acceptons des "travelers checks."
We accept travelers checks.

Clothes

a blouse	a skirt	a woman's suit
un corsage	une jupe	un tailleur
un kor-sazh	*ûne zhûp*	*un ta-yuhr*

1. Pronounce *û* like *ee* with your lips in a tight circle.
2. *zh* is like the *s* in measure.
3. *n* means a nasal "n," pronounced through the nose.

a coat
un manteau
un mahn-to

a hat
un chapeau
un sha-po

a scarf
une écharpe
une ay-sharp

a handbag
un sac
un sak

shoes
des chaussures
day sho-sur

stockings
des bas
day ba

gloves
des gants
day gahn

pajamas
un pyjama
un pee-zha-ma

a nightgown
une chemise de
nuit
*une shuh-meez
duh nwee*

a slip
une combinaison
*une kohn-bee-
nay-sohn*

panties
une culotte
une ku-loht

a brassiere
un soutien-gorge
*un soot-yen
gorzh*

slippers
des pantoufles
day pahn-toofl'

a bathrobe
un peignoir de bain
un pay-nwahr duh ben

an evening dress
une robe du soir
une rohb du swahr

an evening coat
un manteau du soir
un mahn-to du swahr

a raincoat
un imperméable
un nan-pair-may-ahbl'

boots
des bottes
day boht

an umbrella
un parapluie
un pa-ra-plwee

a swimsuit
un costume de bain
un kos-tume duh ben

a shirt
une chemise
une shuh-meez

pants
un pantalon
un pahn-ta-lohn

a jacket
une veste
une vest

a suit	a tie	socks
un complet	une cravate	des chaussettes
un kohn-play	*ûne kra-vaht*	*day sho-set*

undershirt	undershorts
un sous-vêtement	un caleçon
un soo-vet-mähn	*un kahl-sohn*

swim trunks	handkerchiefs
un maillot de bain	des mouchoirs
un ma-yo duh ben	*day moo-shwahr*

Sizes—Colors—Materials

What size?	small	medium
Quelle taille?	petit	moyen
kell ta-yuh?	*puh-tee*	*mwa-yen*

large	extra large	larger
grand	très grand	plus grand
grahn	*tray grahn*	*plû grahn*

smaller	wider	narrower
plus petit	plus large	plus étroit
plû puh-tee	*plû larzh*	*plû zay-trwa*

longer	shorter
plus long	plus court
plû lohn	*plû koor*

What color?	red	blue
De quelle couleur?	rouge	bleu
duh kell koo-luhr?	*roozh*	*bluh*

---

1. *Pronounce* *ŭ* *like* *ee* *with your lips in a tight circle.*
2. *zh* *is like the* *s* *in measure.*
3. *n* *means a nasal "n," pronounced through the nose.*

yellow	orange	green	purple
jaune	orange	vert	violet
zhohn	*o-rahnzh*	*vair*	*vee-o-lay*

brown	gray	tan	black
brun	gris	beige	noir
brun	*gree*	*bayzh*	*nwahr*

white	darker	lighter
blanc	plus foncé	plus clair
blahn	*plù fohn-say*	*plù klair*

Is it silk? wool
C'est de la soie? de la laine
say duh la swah? *duh la lain*

cotton	lace	velvet
du coton	de la dentelle	du velours
dù ko-tohn	*duh la dahn-tel*	*dù vuh-loor*

leather	suede	kid	plastic
du cuir	du daim	du chevreau	du plastique
dù kweer	*dù den*	*dù shuh-vro*	*dù plahss-teek*

fur **What kind of fur?**
de la fourrure Quelle genre de fourrure?
duh la foo-rur *kell zhahnr' duh foo-rùr?*

fox	beaver	mink
du renard	du castor	du vison
dù ruh-nahr	*dù kàhss-tohr*	*dù vee-zohn*

sable **Persian lamb**
de la zibeline de l'astrakan
duh la zeeb-leen *duh lahss-tra-kahn*

Newsstand

I would like a guide book.
Je voudrais un guide.
zhuh voo-dray zuн gheed.

a map of the city.
un plan de la ville.
uн plahн duh la veel

postcards
des cartes postales
day kart pohs-tahl

sunglasses
des lunettes de soleil
day lŭ-net duh so-lay'

this newspaper
ce journal
suh zhoor-nahl

that magazine
ce magazine
suh ma-ga-zeeн

a newspaper in English
un journal en anglais
uн zhoor-nahl ahн nahн-glay

Tobacco Shop

Have you American cigarettes?
Avez-vous des cigarettes américaines?
ah-vay voo day see-ga-ret ah-may-ree-kain?

O.K.
Ça va.
sa va.

I'll take Gauloises.
Je prends des Gauloises.
zhuh prahн day go-lwahz.

cigars
des cigares
day see-gar

a pipe
une pipe
ŭne peep

tobacco
du tabac
dŭ ta-ba

matches
des allumettes
day za-lŭ-met

a lighter
un briquet
uн bree-kay

a lighter refill
un rechange
uн ruh-shahнzh

---

1. *Pronounce ŭ like ee with your lips in a tight circle.*
2. *zh is like the s in measure.*
3. *н means a nasal "n," pronounced through the nose.*

Drugstore

a toothbrush	toothpaste	a razor
une brosse à dents	du dentifrice	un rasoir
ûne brohss ah dahn	*dû dahn-tee-freess*	*un ra-zwahr*

razor blades	shaving cream
des lames de rasoir	de la crème à raser
day lahm duh ra-zwahr	*duh la kraim ah ra-zay*

cologne	a hairbrush	a comb
de l'eau de Cologne	une brosse à cheveux	un peigne
duh lo duh ko-loy'n	*ûne brohss áh shuh-vuh*	*un pain*

aspirin	iodine	an antiseptic
de l'aspirine	de la teinture d'iode	un antiseptique
duh lahs-pee-reen	*duh la tan-tûr dee-ohd*	*un ahn-tee-sep-teek*

scissors	a nailfile	a bandage
des ciseaux	une lime à ongles	des bandages
day see-zo	*ûne leem ah ohngl'*	*day bahn-dazh*

coughdrops
des pastilles pour la toux
day pahs-tee poor la too

Cosmetics

makeup base	powder	lipstick
un fond de teint	de la poudre	un rouge à lèvres
un fohn duh ten	*duh la poodr'*	*un roozh ah levr'*

eye shadow	**mascara**
un crayon à paupières	du mascara
uɴ kray-yohɴ ah pohp-yair	*dů mas-ka-ra*
eyebrow pencil	**cleansing cream**
un crayon à sourcips	de la crème à nettoyer
uɴ kray-yohɴ ah soor-see	*duh la kraim ah nay-twah-yay*
bobby pins	**cotton pads**
des barrettes	des boules de coton
day ba-rett	*day bool duh koh-tohɴ*
perfume	**That smells good, doesn't it?**
du parfum	Ça sent bon, n'est-ce pas?
dů par-feɴ	*sa sahɴ bohɴ, ness pa?*

Hairdresser

a shampoo	**and set**	**a manicure**
un shampooing	et mise en plis	une manucure
uɴ shahɴ-pweɴ	*ay mee-zahɴ plee*	*ůne ma-nů-kůr*
It's too hot.	**a color rinse**	**lighter**
C'est trop chaud.	un rinçage	plus clair
say tro ʒho.	*uɴ reɴ-sahzh*	*plů klair*
darker	**That's good.**	
plus foncé	Ça va.	
plů fohɴ-say	*sa va.*	

Barber

a haircut	**a shave**	**a massage**
une coupe de cheveux	la barbe	un massage
ůne koop duh shuh-vuh	*la bahrb*	*uɴ ma-sazh*

---

1. *Pronounce ů like ee with your lips in a tight circle.*
2. zh *is like the s in measure.*
3. ɴ *means a nasal "n," pronounced through the nose.*

Use scissors.	**Not the clippers.**
Employez les ciseaux.	Pas la tondeuse.
ahn-plwa-yay lay see-zo.	*pa la tohn-duhz.*

shorter	**not too short**	**the top**
plus court	pas trop court	le dessus
plù koor	*pa tro koor*	*luh duh-sù*

in back	**the sides**	**That's fine.**
derrière	les côtés	C'est très bien.
dair-yair	*lay ko-tay*	*say tray b'yen.*

Food Market

I would like . . .	**. . . a dozen of . . .**
Je voudrais . . .	. . . une douzaine de . . .
zhuh voo-dray . . .	*. . . ùne doo-zain duh . . .*

. . . this.	**. . . that.**
. . . ceci.	. . . cela.
. . . suh-see.	*. . . suh-la.*

I want five.	**Is this fresh?**
J'en veux cinq.	C'est bien frais?
zhahn vuh senk.	*say b'yen fray?*

Three cans of this.	**How much per kilo?**
Trois boites de ceci.	C'est combien le kilo?
trwah bwaht duh suh-see.	*say kohn-b'yen luh kee-lo?*

Can one buy wine here?	**Brandy?**
Peut-on acheter du vin ici?	Du cognac?
puh-tohn ash-tay dù ven ee-see?	*dù kohn-yak?*

What is this?
Qu'est-ce que c'est?
kess kuh say?

Put it in a bag, please.
Mettez-le dans un sac, s'il vous plaît.
may-tay-luh dahn zun sak, seel voo play.

En passant: Wine and other alcoholic beverages are generally sold in food stores. Une bonne idée, n'est-ce pas?

Jewelry

I would like . . .	. . . a watch.	. . . a ring.
Je voudrais . . .	. . . une montre.	. . . une bague.
zhuh voo-dray . . .	. . . *üne mohntr'.*	. . . *üne bahg.*

. . . a necklace.	. . . a bracelet.	. . . earrings.
. . . un collier.	. . . un bracelet.	. . . des boucles
. . . *un kohl-yay.*	. . . *un brass-lay.*	d'oreille.
		. . . *day bookl'*
		doh-ray.

Is this gold?	. . . platinum?	. . . silver?
Est-ce de l'or?	. . . du platine?	. . . de l'argent?
ess duh lor?	. . . *dü pla-teen?*	. . . *duh lar-*
		zhahn?

Is it solid or plated?	a diamond
C'est massif ou plaqué?	un diamant
say ma-seef oo pla-kay?	*un dee-ah-mahn*

a pearl	a ruby	a sapphire
une perle	un rubis	un saphir
üne pairl	*un rü-bee*	*un sa-feer*

---

1. *Pronounce ü like ee with your lips in a tight circle.*
2. *zh is like the s in measure.*
3. *n means a nasal "n," pronounced through the nose.*

an amethyst
une améthyste
ûne ah-may-teest

a topaz
une topaz
ûne toh-paz

Antiques

What period is this?
C'est de quelle époque?
say duh kell ay-pohk?

It's beautiful.
C'est beau.
say bo.

But very expensive.
Mais très cher.
may tray shair.

How much (is) . . .
Combien (est) . . .
kohn-b'yen (ay) . . .

. . . this book?
. . . ce livre?
. . . suh leevr'?

. . . this picture?
. . . ce tableau?
. . . suh ta-blo?

. . . this map?
. . . cette carte?
. . . set kart?

. . . this frame?
. . . ce cadre?
. . . suh kahdr'?

. . . this piece of furniture?
. . . ce meuble?
. . . suh muhbl'

Is it an antique?
Est-ce que c'est d'époque?
ess kuh say day-pohk?

Can you ship it?
Pouvez-vous l'expédier?
poo-vay-voo lex-paid-yay?

To this address.
À cette adresse.
ah set ah-dress.

⚜ 17. Telephone

Talking on the telephone is an excellent test of your ability to communicate in French, because you can't see the person you are talking to or use gestures to help get across your meaning. When asking for someone, simply say his name and add **S'il vous plaît.** If you say the number instead of dialing, give it in pairs. For Passy 6066, you would say 60–66: **soixante–soixante-six.**

Where is the telephone?
Où est le téléphone?
oo ay luh tay-lay-fohn?

Hello!
Allô!
ah-lo!

The telephone operator
La téléphoniste
la tay-lay-fo-neest

Operator!
Mademoiselle!
mahd-mwa-zell!

Information
Les renseignements
lay rahn-sayn-mahn

The telephone number of ——.
Le numéro de téléphone de ——.
luh nŭ-may-ro duh tay-lay-fohn duh ——.

Long distance
Interurbain
en-tair-ŭr-ben

Get me, please, number ——.
Donnez-moi, s'il vous plaît, le numéro ——.
do-nay-mwa, seel voo play, luh nŭ-may-ro ——.

---

1. *Pronounce ŭ like ee* with your lips in a tight circle.
2. *zh* is like the *s* in measure.
3. *n* means a nasal "n," pronounced through the nose.

Operator, that was the wrong number.
Mademoiselle, c'était le mauvais numéro.
mahd-mwa-zell, say-tay luh mo-vay nǔ-may-ro.

I want to call Washington, in the United States.
Je veux appeler Washington, aux États-Unis.
zhuh vuh zahp-lay washington, oh zay-ta-zǔ-nee.

The number I am calling is ———.	**Extension ———.**
Le numéro que je demande est ———.	Poste ———.
luh nǔ-may-ro kuh zhuh duh-mahнd ay ———.	*post ———.*

Must I wait long?
Faut-il attendre longtemps?
fo-teel ah-tahнdr' lohн-tahн?

How much is it per minute?	**My number is ———.**
C'est combien la minute?	Mon numéro est ———.
say kohн-b'yeн la mee-nǔt?	*mohн nǔ-may-ro ay ———.*

Mr. Simon, please.
Monsieur Simon, s'il vous plaît.
muss-yuh see-mohн, seel voo play.

What?	**Hold the line!**	**He isn't here.**
Comment?	Ne quittez pas!	Il n'est pas là.
ko-mahн?	*nuh kee-tay pas!*	*eel nay pa la.*

When is he coming back?	**When is she coming back?**
Quand revient-il?	Quand revient-elle?
kahн ruhv-yeн teel?	*kahн ruhv-yeн tell?*

Very well. I'll call back.
Bien. Je rappelerai.
B'yeн. zhuh ra-pel-ray.

Can you take a message?
Pouvez-vous prendre un
   message?
*poo-vay voo prahƞdr
   uƞ may-sazh?*

Ask him (her) to call me.
Demandez-lui de m'appeler.
*duh-mahƞ-day-lwee duh
   mahp-lay.*

At this number: ——.
À ce numéro: ——.
ah suh nǔ-may-ro: ——

Who is speaking?
Qui est à l'appareil?
Kee ay ta la-pa-ray?

This is Mr. Smith calling.
De la part de Monsieur Smith.
duh lah par duh muss-yuh smith.

That is written S-M-I-T-H.
Cela s'écrit S-M-I-T-H.
suh-la say-kree ess-em-ee-tay-ahsh.

A	B	C	D	E	F	G	H
ah	*bay*	*say*	*day*	*uh*	*ef*	*zhay*	*ahsh*

I	J	K	L	M	N	O	P
ee	*zhee*	*kah*	*el*	*em*	*en*	*oh*	*pay*

Q	R	S	T	U	V	W	
kǔ	*air*	*ess*	*tay*	*ǔ*	*vay*	*doo-bl'*	*vay*

X	Y	Z
eeks	*ee grek*	*zed*

En passant: As American and English names are often strange to French ears, you will find the French alphabet very useful for spelling your name when you leave a message.

---

1. *Pronounce ǔ like ee with your lips in a tight circle.*
2. *zh is like the s in measure.*
3. *ƞ means a nasal "n," pronounced through the nose.*

Where is a public telephone?
Où ya-t-il un téléphone public?
oo ee ya teel un tay-lay-fohn pŭ-bleek?

A token, please.
Un jeton, s'il vous plaît.
un zhuh-tohn, seel voo play.

Another token.
Encore un jeton.
ahn-kohr un zhuh-tohn.

Two twenty-centime pieces.
Deux pièces de vingt centimes.
duh p'yes duh ven sahn-teem.

The telephone book.
L'annuaire.
la-nŭ-air.

If there is no public telephone:

May I use your phone?
Je peux me servir de votre téléphone?
zhuh puh muh sair-veer duh votr'. tay-lay-fohn?

Go right ahead.
Je vous en prie.
zuh voo zahn pree.

How much do I owe you?
Qu'est-ce je vous dois?
kess-kuh zhuh voo dwa?

⚜ 18. Post Office and Telegrams

One of the first things you do when abroad is to write postcards—**des cartes postales**—to friends and relatives. Here are the words you will need to know in order to mail them. You might also impress your friends by writing a few words in French, which you will find at the end of this section.

Where is the post office?
Où est le Bureau de Postes?
oo ay luh bů-ro duh post?

Where is the mailbox?
Où est la boîte à lettres?
oo ay la bwaht ah let-tr'?

Ten fifty-centime stamps.
Dix, timbres de cinquante centimes.
dee teн-br' duh seн-kahнt sahн-teem.

How much do I put on? Combien faut-il mettre? *kohн-b'yeн fo-teel met-tr'?*	**Airmail** . . . Par avion . . . *par ahv-yohн* . . .
. . . to Canada. . . . au Canada. *. . . oh ka-na-da.*	**. . . to the United States.** . . . aux Etats-Unis. *. . . oh zay-ta-zů-nee*
. . . to England. . . . en Angleterre. *. . . ahн aнh-gluh-tair.*	**. . . to Australia.** . . . en Australie. *. . . ahн ohss-tra-lee.*

---

1. *Pronounce* ů *like* ee *with your lips in a tight circle.*
2. *zh is like the s in measure.*
3. *н means a nasal "n," pronounced through the nose.*

For names of other countries, see dictionary.

Registered.	**Insured.**
Recommendé.	Assuré.
ruh-ko-mahн-day.	*ah-sû-ray.*

Where can I send a telegram?
Où est-ce que je peux télégraphier?
oo ess kuh zhuh puh tay-lay-graf-yay?

How much is it per word?
C'est combien le mot?
say kohн-b'yeн luh mo?

I need . . . writing paper.	**. . . envelopes.**
J'ai besoin . . .	. . . d'enveloppes.
de papier à lettres.	. . . *dahн-vuh-lohp.*
zhay buh-sweн . . .	
duh pap-yay ah lettr'.	

Can you lend me . . .	**. . . a pen?**
Pouvez-vous me prêter . . .	. . . un stylo?
poo-vay-voo muh pray-tay . . .	. . . *uн stee-lo?*

. . . some stamps?	**. . . a pencil?**
. . . des timbres?	. . . un crayon?
. . . *day teн-br'?*	. . . *uн kray-yohн?*

Dear John,	**Dear Jane,**
Mon cher Jean,	Ma chère Jeanne,
mohн shair zhahн,	*Ma shair zhahn,*

I miss you.	**Best regards from Nice.**
Vous me manquez.	Bons souvenirs de Nice.
voo muh mahн-kay.	*bohн soov-neer duh neece.*

Best wishes to everyone.	**All the best.**
Amitiés à tout le monde.	Bien à vous.
ah-meet-yay ah tool-mohнd.	*b'yeн nah voo.*

⚜ 19. Seasons and the Weather

winter	spring	summer	autumn
l'hiver	le printemps	l'été	l'automne
lee-vair	*luh pren-tahn*	*lay-tay*	*lo-tonn*

How is the weather?
Quel temps fait-il?
kel tahn fay-teel?

The weather is fine.
Il fait beau.
eel fay bo.

It's very hot.
Il fait très chaud.
eel fay tray sho.

It's cold.
Il fait froid.
eel fay frwah.

It's raining.
Il pleut.
eel pluh.

Let's go swimming.
Allons nager.
ah-lohn na-zhay.

Where is the pool?
Où est la piscine?
oo ay la pee-seen?

I need . . . an umbrella.
J'ai besoin . . . d'un parapluie.
zhay buh-zwen . . . dun pa-ra-plwee.

. . . boots.
. . . de bottes.
. . . duh boht.

. . . a raincoat.
. . . d'un imperméable.
. . . dun nen-pair-may-abl'.

What a fog!
Quel brouillard!
kel broo-yahr!

One can't see anything.
On n'y voit rien.
on nee vwa r'yen.

---

1. *Pronounce ŭ like ee with your lips in a tight circle.*
2. *zh is like the s in measure.*
3. *n means a nasal "n," pronounced through the nose.*

It's snowing.
Il neige.
eel nayzh.

Do you like to ski?
Aimez-vous faire du ski?
ay-may-voo fair dŭ ski?

I want to rent skis.
Je voudrais louer des skis.
zhuh voo-dray loo-ay day skee.

Where's the tow?
Où est le remonte-pente?
oo ay luh ruh-mohnt-pahnt?

En passant: Temperature is expressed in centigrade, not Fahrenheit. Zero is freezing in centigrade, and 100° is boiling. To change centigrade to Fahrenheit, multiply by 9/5 and add 32°. To change Fahrenheit to centigrade, subtract 32° and multiply by 5/9.

⚜ 20. Doctor and Dentist

Doctor

I am ill.
Je suis malade.
zhuh swee ma-lahd.

My wife is sick.
Ma femme est malade.
ma fahm ay ma-lahd.

My husband is ill.
Mon mari est malade.
mohн ma-ree ay ma-lahd.

My child is ill.
Mon enfant est malade.
mohн nahн fahн ay ma-lahd.

My friend is ill.
Mon ami est malade.
mohн na-mee ay ma-lahd.

I need a doctor.
J'ai besoin d'un médecin.
zhay buh-zweн d'uн maid-seн.

When can he come here?
Quand peut-il venir?
kahн puh-teel vuh-neer?

Well, what's wrong with you?
Bien, qu'est-ce que vous avez?
b'yeн, kess kuh voo za-vay?

I don't feel well.
Je ne me sens pas bien.
zhuh nuh muh sahн pa b'yeн.

Where does it hurt?
Où avez-vous mal?
oo ah-vay-voo mahl?

Here.
Ici.
ee-see.

---

1. *Pronounce ů like ee with your lips in a tight circle.*
2. *zh is like the s in measure.*
3. *н means a nasal "n," pronounced through the nose.*

I have a pain . . .   . . . in my head.   . . . in the throat.
J'ai mal . . .   . . . à la tête.   . . . à la gorge.
zhay mahl . . .   *. . . ah la tet.*   *. . . ah la gorzh.*

. . . in the ear.   . . . in the stomach.   . . . in the back.
. . . à l'oreille.   . . . à l'estomac.   . . . au dos.
. . . ah lohr-ay.   *. . . ah lay-sto-ma.*   *. . . oh doh.*

I hurt . . .   . . . my leg.   . . . my foot.
Je me suis fait   . . . à la jambe.   . . . au pied.
  mal . . .   *. . . ah la-*   *. . . oh p'yay.*
zhuh muh swee   *zhahnb'.*
  fay mahl . . .

. . . my arm.   . . . my ankle.   . . . my hand.
. . . au bras.   . . . à la cheville.   . . . à la main.
. . . oh bra.   *. . . ah la shuh-*   *. . . ah la men.*
      veel.

I am dizzy.   I have fever.
J'ai le vertige.   J'ai de la fièvre.
zhay luh vair-teezh.   *zhay duh la' f'yevr'.*

I can't sleep.   I have diarrhea.
Je ne peux pas dormir.   J'ai la diarrhée.
zhuh nuh puh pa dohr-meer.   *zhay la d'ya-ray.*

Since when?   Since yesterday.
Depuis quand?   Depuis heir.
duh-pwee kahn?   *duh-pwee yair.*

Since two days ago.   What have you eaten?
Depuis deux jours.   Qu'est-ce que vous avez mangé?
duh-pwee duh zhoor.   *kess kuh voo za-vay mahn-zhay?*

Undress.   Lie down.   Sit up.
Déshabillez-vous.   Couchez-vous.   Redressez-vous.
day-za-bee-yay   *koo-shay-voo.*   *ruh-dray-say-*
  voo.   *voo.*

Breathe deeply.
Respirez profondément.
ress-pee-ray pro-fohn-day-mahn.

Open your mouth.
Ouvrez la bouche.
oo-vray la boosh.

Show me your tongue.
Tirez la langue.
tee-ray la lahng.

Cough.
Toussez.
too-say.

Get dressed again.
Rabillez-vous.
ra-bee-yay-voo.

It is necessary to ...
Il faut ...
eel fo ...

... stay in bed.
... rester au lit.
... ress-tay oh lee.

... go to the hospital.
... aller à l'hôpital.
... tah-lay ah lo-pee-tahl.

... take these pills.
... prendre ces pillules.
... prahndr' say pee-lul'.

... take this prescription.
... suivre cette ordonnance.
... sweevr' set ohr-doh-nahnss.

Is it serious?
C'est grave?
say grahv?

Don't worry.
Ne vous en faites pas.
nuh voo zahn fett pa.

It's not serious.
Ce n'est pas grave.
suh nay pa grahv.

You have ...
Vous avez ...
voo za-vay ...

... indigestion.
... une indigestion.
... üne en-dee-zhest-yohn.

---

1. *Pronounce* ü *like* ee *with your lips in a tight circle.*
2. *zh is like the* s *in measure.*
3. *n means a nasal "n," pronounced through the nose.*

... an infection.
... une infection.
... ûne en-fex-yohn.

... a cold.
... un rhume.
... un rûme.

... a heart attack.
... une crise cardiaque.
... ûne kreez kard-yahk.

... appendicitis.
... une appendicite.
... ûne a-pahn-dee-seet.

... liver trouble
... une crise de foie.
... ûne kreez duh fwa.

Be careful.
Attention.
ah-tahn-syohn.

Don't eat too much.
Ne mangez pas trop.
nuh mahn-zhay pa tro.

Don't drink any alcohol.
Ne buvez pas d'alcool.
nuh bû-vay pa dahl-kohl.

Except wine, naturally.
Sauf du vin, naturellement.
*sohf dû ven, na-tûr-rel-
mahn.*

How is it going today?
Comment ça va aujourd'hui?
ko-mahn sa va oh-zhoor-dwee?

Badly.
Mal.
mahl.

Better.
Mieux.
m'yuh.

Much better.
Beaucoup mieux.
bo-koo m'yuh.

En passant: The centigrade scale is also used to measure body temperature (See p.126) The normal body temperature is 36.7 degrees. So if you have anything higher than this, you have fever—Vous avez de la fièvre.

Dentist

In the unlikely event that the dentist should hurt you, tell him "Stop!"—**Arrêtez!**—or "Wait a minute!"—**Attendez une minute!** This will give you time to regain your courage.

Can you recommend a dentist?
Pouvez-vous recommander un dentiste?
poo-vay voo ruh-ko-mahn-day un dahn-teest?

I have a toothache.
J'ai mal aux dents.
zhay mahl oh dahn.

It hurts here.
J'ai mal là.
zhay mahl la.

You need a filling.
Il vous faut un plombage.
eel voo fo tun plohn-bahzh.

There is an infection.
Il y a de l'infection.
eel ee ya duh len-fex-yohn.

The tooth must come out.
Il faut arracher cette dent.
eel fo ta-ra-shay set dahn.

Will it take long?
Est-ce que ce sera long?
ess kuh suh suh-ra lohn?

Just fix it temporarily.
Arrangez-la temporairement.
ah-rahn-zhay-la tahn-po-rair-mahn.

An injection against pain, please.
Une piqûre contre la douleur, s'il vous plaît.
ûne pee-kûr kohn-tr' la doo-lurr, seel voo play.

---

1. *Pronounce* û *like* ee *with your lips in a tight circle.*
2. *zh is like the* s *in measure.*
3. *n means a nasal "n," pronounced through the nose.*

Does it hurt?	Yes, a little.	Not at all.
Ça fait mal?	Oui, un peu.	Pas du tout.
sa fay mahl?	*wee, uɴ puh.*	*pa dŭ too.*

Is it finished?	How much do I owe you?
C'est fini?	Combien je vous dois?
say fee-nee?	*kohɴ-b'yeɴ zhuh voo dwa?*

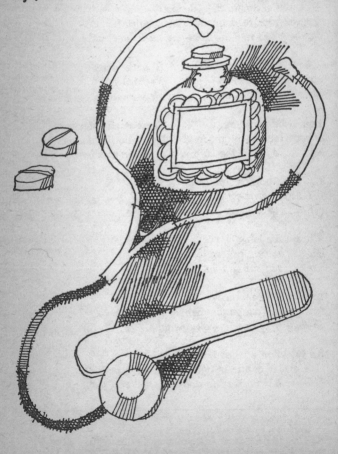

⚜ 21. Problems and Police

Although the situations suggested below may never happen to you, the words are useful to know, just in case.

Go away!
Allez-vous en!
ah-lay voo zahn!

Leave me alone.
Laissez-moi tranquille.
lay-say mwah trahn-keel.

. . . or I'll call a policeman.
. . . ou j'appelle un agent.
. . . oo zha-pel un na-zhahn.

Police!
Police!
po-leess!

What's going on?
Qu'est-ce qui se passe?
kess kee suh pahss?

This man is following me.
Cet homme me poursuit.
set ohm muh poor-swee.

Where is the police station?
Où est le commissariat de police?
oo ay luh ko-mee-sahr-ya duh po-leess?

I have been robbed of . . .
On m'a volé . . .
ohn ma vo-lay . . .

. . . my wallet.
. . . mon portefeuille.
. . . mohn port-foy.

. . . my car.
. . . ma voiture.
. . . ma vwa-tŭr.

. . . my watch.
. . . ma montre.
. . . ma mohn-tr'.

. . . my jewelry.
. . . mes bijoux.
. . . may bee-zhoo.

. . . my suitcase
. . . ma valise
. . . ma va-leez.

... my passport.
... mon passeport.
... *mohn pass-pohr.*

Stop thief!
Au voleur!
oh vo-lurr!

Stop that man!	**Wait!**	**That's the one!**
Arrêtez cet homme!	Attendez!	C'est celui-là!
ah-ray-tay set ohm!	*ah-tahn-day!*	*say suh-lwee-la.*

Do you wish to make a complaint?
Voulez-vous porter plainte?
voo-lay-voo pohr-tay plent?

I don't recognize him.
. Je ne le reconnais pas.
zhuh nuh luh ruh-ko-nay pa.

I haven't done anything.
Je n'ai rien fait.
zhuh nay r'yen fay.

I am innocent..
Je suis innocent.
zhuh swee zee-no-sahn.

I need a lawyer.
J'ai besoin d'un avocat.
zhay buh-zwen dun na-vo-ka.

Notify the American consul.
Prévenez le Consul des États-Unis.
pray-v'nay luh kohn-sul day zay-ta-zŭ-nee.

It's nothing.
Ce n'est rien.
suh nay r'yen.

It is a misunderstanding.
C'est un malentendu.
say tun ma-lahn-tahn-dŭ.

Don't worry.
Ne vous en faites pas.
nuh voo zahn fett pa.

Can I go now?
Puis-je partir maintenant?
pweezh par-teer ment-nahn?

---

1. *Pronounce ŭ like ee with your lips in a tight circle.*
2. *zh is like the s in measure.*
3. *n means a nasal "n," pronounced through the nose.*

⚜ 22. Housekeeping

The following chapter will be especially interesting for those who to stay for a time in France or have occasion to employ French-speaking babysitters or household help, abroad or even at home.

What is your name?
Comment vous appelez-vous?
ko-mahn voo zahp-lay-voo?

Where have you worked before?
Où avez-vous travaillé avant?
oo ah-vay-voo tra-va-yay ah-vahn?

Can you take care of a baby?
Savez-vous vous occuper d'un bébé?
sa-vay-voo voo zo-kŭ-pay dun bay-bay?

Do you know how to cook?
Savez-vous faire la cuisine?
sa-vay-voo fair la kwee-zeen?

This is your room.
Voici votre chambre.
vwa-see votr' shahnbr'.

Thursday will be your day off.
Le jeudi sera votre jour de congé.
luh zhuh-dee suh-ra votr' zhoor duh kohn-zhay.

We will pay you ———— per week.
Nous vous paierons ———— par semaine.
noo voo pay-rohn ———— par suh-men.

---

1. *Pronounce ŭ* like *ee* with your lips in a tight circle.
2. *zh* is like the *s* in measure.
3. *n* means a nasal "n," pronounced through the nose.

Please clean . . .
Nettoyez, s'il vous plaît . . .
nay-twa-yay, seel voo play . . .

. . . the living room.
. . . le salon.
. . . luh sa-lohn.

. . . the dining room.
. . . la salle à manger.
. . . la sahl ah mahn-zhay.

. . . the bedroom.
. . . la chambre.
. . . la shahnbr'.

. . . the bathroom.
. . . la salle de bain.
. . . la sahl duh ben.

. . . the kitchen.
. . . la cuisine.
. . . la kwee-zeen.

Wash the dishes.
Faites la vaisselle.
fett la vay-sell.

Sweep the floor.
Balayez le plancher.
ba-lay-yay luh plahn-shay.

Use the vacuum cleaner.
Prenez l'aspirateur.
pruh-nay lahss-pee-ra-turr.

. . . the broom.
. . . le balai.
. . . luh ba-lay.

Polish the silver.
Faites l'argenterie.
fett lahr-zhahnt-ree.

Have you finished?
Avez-vous fini?
ah-vay voo fee-nee?

Make the beds.
Faites les lits.
fett lay lee.

Change the sheets.
Changez les draps.
shahn-zhay lay dra.

Wash this.
Lavez ceci.
la-vay suh-see.

Use bleach.
Mettez de l'eau de Javel.
may-tay duh lo duh zha-vel.

Iron that.
Repassez cela.
ruh-pa-say suh-la.

Mend this.
Recousez ceci.
ruh-koo-zay suh-see.

What do we need?
De quoi avons-nous besoin?
duh kwa ah-vohn-noo buh-zwen?

Go to the market.
Allez au marché.
ah-lay oh mar-shay.

Here is the list.
Voici la liste.
vwa-see la leest.

Put the milk in the refrigerator.
Mettez le lait au frigidaire.
may-tay luh lay oh free-zhee-dair.

If someone calls, write the name here.
Si quelqu'un appelle, écrivez le nom ici.
see kel-kuн ah-pell, ay-kree-vay luh nohн ee-see.

I'll be at this number.
Je serai à ce numéro.
zhuh suh-ray ah suh nů-may-ro.

I'll be back at 4 o'clock.
Je serai de retour à quatre heures.
zhuh suh-ray duh ruh-toor ah katr' urr.

Give the baby a bottle at ————.
Donnez un biberon au bébé à ————.
doh-nay uн beeb-rohн oh bay-bay ah ————.

Give the child a bath.
Donnez un bain à l'enfant.
doh-nay zuн beн ah lahн-fahн.

Put him to bed at ————.
Mettez-le au lit à ————.
may-tay-luh oh lee ah ————.

---

1. *Pronounce* ů *like* ee *with your lips in a tight circle.*
2. *zh is like the s in measure.*
3. *н means a nasal "n," pronounced through the nose.*

Did anyone call?
Est-ce que quelqu'un a téléphoné?
ess-kuh kell-kun ah tay-lay-fo-nay?

Serve lunch at 1 o'clock.
Servez le déjeuner à une heure.
sair-vay luh day-zhuh-nay ah ûne urr.

There will be guests this evening.
Il y aura des invités ce soir.
eel ee oh-ra day zen-vee-tay suh swahr.

Serve dinner at 9 o'clock.
Servez le dîner à neuf heures.
sair-vay luh dee-nay ah nuh vurr.

⚜ 23. A New Type of Dictionary

The following dictionary supplies a list of English words and their translation into French, which will enable you to make up your own sentences in addition to those given in the phrase book. By using these words, in conjunction with the following advice and shortcuts, you will be able to make up hundreds of sentences by yourself. Only one French equivalent is given for each English word—the one most useful to you—so you won't be in any doubt regarding which word to use. Every word in this dictionary is followed by the phonetic pronunciation, so you will have no difficulty being understood.

All French nouns are either masculine or feminine, and the adjective that goes with the noun (usually following it) must be masculine or feminine as well. In this dictionary (m) denotes a masculine noun and (f) a feminine one. The feminine of adjectives is usually formed by adding an *e:*

the green suit **le costume vert**
  (Le is the masculine form of "the.")
the green dress **la robe verte**
  (La is the feminine form of "the.")
  (Le or la becomes l' before a noun starting with a vowel.)

When two forms are given in the dictionary for an adjective, the first is masculine and the second is feminine.

Plurals are generally formed by adding s, or sometimes x. When the plural ends in x, this will be indicated in the dictionary.

the green dresses **les robes vertes**
  (Les is the plural form of "the" for both masculine and feminine.)

French verbs change their forms according to the pronouns used with them. The most important forms you will need for each verb are given within the different sections of the phrase book. To help you make up your own sentences, the present tense forms for "to be," "to have," "to come," "to go," and "to want" are given in the dictionary.

The verbs in the dictionary are in the infinitive form, and change their ending according to the subject. Although a full grammatical explanation is not within the scope of this book, the following table will help you to use and recognize the important present tense forms of most of the verbs in the dictionary.

Verbs are divided in three groups, according to their infinitive endings: verbs in -er form the first group; those in ir the second; and those in -re and -oir together form the third group. **Parler** (to speak) and **finir** (to finish) are examples of the first and second groups; **perdre** (to lose) and **recevoir** (to receive) are examples of the third group. Most French verbs belong to the first group. Each verb has six forms in each tense. Here is the present tense of **parler** (to speak) with its English equivalents:

je parle	I speak *or* I am speaking
tu parles	you speak *or* you are speaking (familiar)
il, elle parle	he, she speaks *or* he, she is speaking
nous parlons	we speak *or* we are speaking
vous parlez	you speak *or* you are speaking (formal)
ils, elles parlent	they speak *or* they are speaking (masc. or fem.)

We have not indicated a pronoun for "it" because, in French, every noun is either masculine or feminine; therefore, "it" is either "he" or "she."

Tu and vous both mean "you." However, you should use vous, the polite form. Tu, the familiar form, is used within the family, between close friends, among students, and to children.

The six forms for the present tense of the second and third verb groups are:

finir: je finis, tu finis, il finit, nous finissons, vous finissez, ils finissent

perdre: je perds, tu perds, il perd, nous perdons, vous perdez, ils perdent

recevoir: je reçois, tu reçois, il reçoit, nous recevons, vous recevez, ils reçoivent

(The little hook under the *c* means that it is pronounced like an *s*.)

You can do a lot of communicating by using simply the present tense. But, in addition, you can use the infinitive to express a variety of other concepts. To say something must be done or is necessary, use il faut directly with the infinitive (that is, the form given in the dictionary):

> I must leave. Il faut partir.

To say you want to do something, use the appropriate form of "want" with the infinitive of the verbs expressing what you want to do:

> I want to leave. Je veux partir.

For the negative, put ne and pas around the verb:

> I don't want to leave. Je ne veux pas partir.

An easy way to give a command or make a request is to say, "Do you want . . ." ("Will you . . .")—Voulez-vous . . .—followed by an infinitive:

> Will you come in? Voulez-vous entrer?

In any case, the imperative is not difficult. It is the same form as that used for "you"—vous—but *without* the pronoun:

> You are leaving. Vous partez.
> Leave! Partez!

An easy way to express what will happen in the future is to use a form of aller (to go) with the next verb in the infinitive:

He is going to buy a ticket. **Il va acheter un billet.**

To form the past tense of the majority of the verbs given in the dictionary, use the present tense of "to have" —avoir—with the past participle:

I have been (I was) **J'ai été**

Since only the most important or irregular past participles are given in the dictionary, note how the past participles are formed for the three groups of French verbs whose infinitives end in -er, -ir, -re, or -oir:

	"to speak"	"to finish"	"to sell"	"to receive"
infinitive:	parler	finir	vendre	recevoir
past participle:	parlé	fini	vendu	reçu

To make the past, use the present of **avoir** with the past participle of the verb you wish to use in the past:

I spoke. (I have spoken.) **J'ai parlé.**

Some verbs use "to be"—être—for the past tense. These are usually the ones that express coming, going, arriving, leaving, etc.:

He has left. (He left). **Il est parti.**

The possessive is always expressed by "of"—de:

Robert's car **la voiture de Robert**

Possessive pronouns are listed in the dictionary.

Object pronouns are given in the dictionary. In a sentence the object pronoun is placed before the verb.

I see her. **Je la vois.**
Do you understand me? **Me comprenez-vous?**
I speak to him. **Je lui parle.**
Don't speak to her. **Ne lui parlez pas.**

French is full of contractions. "To the"—à plus **le**, **la**, or **les**—becomes **au**, **à la** and **aux** respectively. "Of the" is **de** plus the definite articles **le**, **la** and **les** and becomes **du**,

de la and des. (These combinations can also mean "some.")
The ubiquitous little words y and en substitute for phrases
made with à and de; y stands for à plus a noun, and en
stands for de plus a noun.

With this advice and the suggestions given within the
dictionary itself, you will be able to make up countless
sentences on your own and to converse with anyone you
may meet.

There is, of course, much more to French than these
few indications we have given you—including the subtleties
of the French verb, the use of partitives, pronouns, contractions, the use of prepositions with verbs, and the
numerous idioms, sayings, and references that reflect the
spirit, wisdom, wit, and history of France. But you can
effectively use this selected basic vocabulary as an important step, or even a springboard, to enter the wonderful
world that is the French heritage and, by constant practice, absorb and improve your command of this beautiful
language. For, as the French say, "Appetite comes with
eating." **L'appétit vient en mangeant.** Once you see how
easy and how rewarding it is to speak to people in French,
you will have the impetus to progress further.

A

a	un, une	*un, ûne*
(to be) able See "can."	pouvoir	*poo-vwahr*
about (concerning)	concernant	*kohn-sair-nahn*

about (approxi- mately)	environ	*ahʀ-vee-rohʀ*
above	au-dessus de	*oh-des-sù duh·*
accent	accent (m)	*ak-sàhʀ*
(to) accept	accepter	*ak-sep-tay*
accident	accident (m)	*ak-see-dahʀ*
account	compte (m)	*kohʀt*
across	de l'autre côté de	*duh lohtr' ko-tay duh*
actor	acteur (m)	*ak-turr*
actress	actrice (f)	*:ak-treess*
address	adresse (f)	*ah-dress*
adjective	adjectif (m)	*ad-zhek-teef*
admission	entrée (f)	*ahʀ-tray*
advertisement·	annonce (f)	*ah-nohʀs*
adverb	adverbe (m)	*ad-vairb*
advice	conseil (m)	*kohʀ-say'*
(to be) afraid	avoir peur	*ah-vwahr purr*
Africa	Afrique (f)	*ah-freek*
African	africain, -e	*ah-free-keʀ, -kain*
after	après	*ah-pray*
afternoon	après-midi (m)	*ah-pray-mee-dee*
again	encore	*ahʀ-kor*
against	contre	*kohʀtr'*
age	âge (m)	*azh*
agency	agence (f)	*ah-zhahʀss*

agent	agent (m)	*ah-zhahn*
ago	il y a	*eel ee ya*
(See p. 34.)		
agreed	entendu	*ahn-tahn-dŭ*
ahead	en avant	*ahn na-vahn*
air	air (m)	*air*
air conditioned	climatisé, -e	*klee-ma-tee-zay*
(by) air mail	par avion	*par-av-yohn*
airplane	avion (m)	*av-yohn*
airport	aéroport (m)	*ah-ay-ro-por*
all	tout, toute	*too, toot*
That's all!	C'est tout!	*say too!*
all right!	Très bien!	*tray b'yen!*
(to) allow	permettre	*pair-metr'*
almost	presque	*presk'*
alone	seul, -e	*sull*
already	déjà	*day-zha*
also	aussi	*oh-see*
always	toujours	*too-zhoor*
(I) am	je suis	*zhuh swee*
ambulance	ambulance (f)	*ahn-bŭ-lahnss*
America	Amérique (f)	*ah-may-reek*
American	américain, -e	*ah-may-ree-ken, -kain*
amusing	amusant, -e	*ah-mŭ-zahn,-zahnt*
and	et	*ay*

angel	ange (m)	*ahnzh*
angry	fâché	*fa-shay*
animal	animal (m)	*ah-nee-mahl*
ankle	cheville (f)	*shuh-vee*
annoying	ennuyeux, -euse	*ahn-nwee-yuh, -yuhz*
another	un autre, une autre	*un nohtr', ûne ohtr'*
answer	réponse (f)	*ray-pohnss*
any (adj.)	quelque	*kelk'*
any (pronoun)	en	*ahn*
anyone	quelqu'un, -e	*kel-kun, -kûn*
anythin	quelque chose	*kel-kuh-shohz*
anywhere	n'importe où	*nen-port-oo*
apartment	appartement (m)	*ah-par-tuh-mahn*
apple	pomme (f)	*pom*
appointment	rendez-vous (m)	*rahn-day-voo*
April	avril (m)	*ah-vreel*
Arab, Arabic	Arabe (m or f)	*ah-rahb*
architecture	architecture (f)	*ar-shee-tek-tûr*
are		
you are	vous êtes	*voo zet*
we are	nous sommes	*noo som*
they (m) are	ils sont	*eel sohn*

they (f) are	elles sont	*el sohn*
there are	il y a	*eel ee ya*
arm	bras (m)	*bra*
army	armée (f)	*ar-may*
around here	par ici	*par ee-see*
(to) arrive	arriver	*ah-ree-vay*
art	art (m)	*ahr*
artist	artiste (m or f)	*ar-teest*
as	comme	*kom*
ashtray	cendrier (m)	*sahn-dree-yay*
Asia	Asie	*ah-zee*
(to) ask	demander	*duh-mahn-day*
asleep	endormi, -e	*ahn-dor-mee*
asparagus	asperge (f)	*ass-pairzh*
aspirin	aspirine (f)	*ass-pee-reen*
assortment	assortiment (m)	*ah-sor-tee-mahn*
at	à	*ah*
Atlantic	Atlantique (m)	*at-lahn-teek*
atomic	atomique	*ah-to-meek*
attractive	joli, -e	*zho-lee*
August	août	*oo*
aunt	tante (f)	*tahnt*
Australia	Australie (f)	*ohss-tra-lee*
Australian	australien, -ne	*ohss-tral-yen, -yen*
Austria	Autriche (f)	*o-treesh*

author	auteur (m or f)	*o-turr*
automatic	automatique	*o-toh-ma-teek*
automobile	automobile (f)	*o-toh-mo-beel*
autumn	automne (m)	*o-tohn*
available	disponible	*dees-po-neebl'*
aviation	aviation (f)	*av-yas-yohn*
avoid	éviter	*ay-vee-tay*
away	absent, -e	*ab-sahn, -sahnt*

B

baby	bébé (m)	*bay-bay*
bachelor	célibataire (m)	*say-lee-ba-tair*
back (part of body)	dos (m)	*doh*
bacon	bacon (m)	*ba-kohn*
bad	*mauvais, -e*	*mo-vay, -vaiz*
That's too bad!	C'est dommage!	*say doh-mazh!*
baggage	bagage (m)	*ba-gazh*
banana	banane (f)	*ba-nahn*
bandage	bandage (m)	*bahn-dazh*
bank	banque (f)	*bahnk*
bar	bar (m)	*bar*
barber	coiffeur (m)	*kwa-furr*
basement	sous-sol (m)	*soo-sol*

basket	panier (m)	*pan-yay*
bath	bain (m)	*ben*
bathing suit	maillot de bain (m)	*ma-yo duh ben*
bathroom	salle de bain (f)	*sal duh ben*
battery	batterie (f)	*.baht-ree*
battle	bataille (f)	*ba-tye*
(to) be	être	*etr'*

(See also "am," "is," "are," "was," "were," "been.")

beach	plage (f)	*plazh*
beans	haricots (m.pl.)	*ah-ree-ko*
bear	ours (m)	*oorss*
beard	barbe (f)	*barb*
beautiful	beau, belle	*bo, bel*
beauty	beauté (f)	*bo-tay*
beauty shop	salon de beauté (m)	*sa-lohn duh bo-tay*
because	parce que	*par-suh-kuh*
bed	lit	*lee*
bedroom	chambre (f)	*shahnbr'*
bedspread	dessus de lit (m)	*duh-sù duh lee*
beef	boeuf (m)	*buhf*
been	été	*ay-tay*
I have been	j'ai été	*zhay ay-tay*
beer	bière (f)	*b'yair*

before (time)	avant	*ah-vahn*
(to) begin	commencer	*ko-mahn-say*
behind	derrière	*dair-yair*
(to) believe	croire	*.krwahr*
belt	ceinture (f)	*sen-tŭr*
besides	d'ailleurs	*da-yuhr*
best (adv)	le mieux	*luh m'yuh*
(adj)	le meilleur, la meilleure	*luh, la may-yurr*
better	meilleur, -e	*may-yurr*
between	entre	*ahntr'*
bicycle	bicyclette (f)	*bee-see-klett*
big	gros, -se	*gro, grohss*
bill	note (f)	*noht*
bird	oiseau (m)	*wa-zo*
birthday	anniver- saire (m)	*ah-nee-vair-sair*
black	noir, -e	*nwahr*
blond	blond, -e	*blohn, blohnd*
blood	sang (m)	*sahn*
blue	bleu	*bluh*
boat	bateau (m)	*ba-toh*
body	corps (m)	*kor*
book	livre (m)	*leevr'*
bookstore	librairie (f)	*lee-bray-ree*
born	né	*nay*

(to) borrow	emprunter	*ahn-prun-tay*
boss	patron (m)	*pa-tron*
both	tous les deux, toutes les deux	*too, toot lay duh*
bottle	bouteille (f)	*boo-tay*
bottom	fond (m)	*fohn*
bought	acheté	*ash-tay*
boy	garçon (m)	*gahr-sohn*
brain	cerveau (m)	*sair-vo*
brake	frein (m)	*fren*
brave	brave	*brahv*
bread	pain (m)	*pen*
(to) break	casser	*ka-say*
breakfast	petit déjeuner (m)	*puh-tee day-zhuh-nay*
(to) breathe	respirer	*res-pee-ray*
bridge	pont (m)	*pohn*
briefcase	serviette	*sair-v'yet*
(to) bring	apporter	*ah-por-tay*
Bring me ...	Apportez-moi ...	*ah-por-tay-mwa ...*
broken	cassé	*ka-say*
brother	frère (m)	*frair*
brother-in-law	beau-frère (m)	*bo-frair*
brown	brun, brune	*brun, brune*
brunette	brune (f)	*brune*

(to) build	construire	*kohn-strweer*
building	bâtiment (m)	*ba-tee-mahn*
built	construit	*kohn-strwee*
bureau	bureau (m)	*bŭ-ro*
bus	autobus (m)	*oh-toh-bŭss*
bus stop	arrêt de l'auto- bus (m)	*ah-ray duh lo-toh-bŭss*
business	les affaires (f. pl)	*lay za-fair*
busy	très occupé	*tray zo-kŭ-pay*
but	mais	*may*
butter	beurre (m)	*burr*
button	bouton (m)	*boo-tohn*
(to) buy	acheter	*ash-tay*
by	par	*par*

C

cab	taxi (m)	*tak-see*
cabbage	chou (m)	*shoo*
cake	gâteau (m)	*ga-toh*
(to) call	appeler	*ap-lay*
Call me.	Appelez-moi.	*ap-lay-mwa.*
camera	appareil photo- graphique (m)	*ah-pa-ray fo-toh-gra- feek*
movie	caméra (f)	*ka-may-ra*

can (be able)	pouvoir	*poo-vwahr*
I can	je peux	*zhuh puh*
you can	vous pouvez	*voo poo-vay*
he can	il peut	*eel puh*
she can	elle peut	*el puh*
we can	nous pouvons	*noo poo-vohn*
they (m) can	ils peuvent	*eel puhv*
they (f) can	elles peuvent	*el puhv*
Can you?	Pouvez-vous?	*poo-vay-voo?*
I can't.	Je ne peux pas.	*zhuh nuh puh pa.*
can (container)	boîte (f)	*bwaht*
can opener	ouvre-boîte (m)	*oovr'-bwaht*
candy	bonbon (m)	*bohn-bohn*
cap	casquette (f)	*kas-ket*
cape	cape (f)	*kahp*
captain	capitaine	*ka-pee-tain*
car	auto (f)	*oh-toh*
carburetor	carburateur (m)	*kar-bŭ-ra-turr*
card	carte (f)	*kart*
(Be) careful!	Faites attention!	*fet ah-tahns-yohn*
carrot	carotte (f)	*ka-rot*
(to) carry	porter	*por-tay*
Carry this to . . .	Portez cela à . . .	*por-tay suh-la ah . . .*

cashier	caissier (m), -ière (f)	*kess-yay, -yair*
castle	chateau (m)	*sha-toh*
cat	chat (m)	*sha*
cathedral	cathédrale (f)	*ka-tay-drahl*
catholic	catholique	*ka-toh-leek*
cemetery	cimetière (m)	*seem-t'yair*
cent	centime (m)	*sahн-teem*
center	centre (m)	*sahнţŗ'*
century	siècle (m)	*s'yekĺ*
certainly	certainement	*sair-tain-mahн*
chair	chaise (f)	*shaiz*
chandelier	lustre (m)	*lûstr'*
change	de la monnaie (f)	*duh la mo-nay*
(to) change	échanger	*ay-shahн-zhay*
charming	charmant, -e	*shar-mahн, -mahнt*
chauffeur	chauffeur (m)	*sho-furr*
cheap	bon marché	*bohн mar-shay*
check	chèque (m)	*shek*
checkroom	vestiaire (m)	*vest-yair*
cheese	fromage (m)	*fro-mazh*
cherries	cerises (f. pl)	*suh-reez*
chest (part of the body)	poitrine (f)	*pwa-treen*
chicken	poulet (m)	*poo-lay*

child	enfant (m or f)	*ahn-fahn*
China	Chine (f)	*sheen*
Chinese	chinois (m), -oise (f)	*sheen-wa, -wahz*
chocolate	chocolat (m)	*sho-ko-la*
chop	côtelette (f)	*koht-let*
church	église (f)	*ay-gleez*
cigar	cigare (m)	*see-gar*
cigarette	cigarette (f)	*see-ga-ret*
city	ville (f)	*veel*
(to) clean	nettoyer	*nay-twa-yay*
clear	clair	*klair*
climate	climat (m)	*klee-ma*
close	près	*pray*
(to) close	fermer	*fair-may*
closed	fermé	*fair-may*
clothes	vêtements (m. pl)	*vett-mahn*
coast	côte (f)	*koht*
coat (overcoat)	manteau (m)	*mahn-toh*
(of suit)	veste (f)	*vest*
coffee	café (m)	*ka-fay*
coin	pièce (m)	*p'yess*
cold	froid, -e	*frwah, frwahd*
college	université (f)	*ŭ-nee-vair-see-tay*
colonel	colonel (m)	*ko-lo-nel*

color	couleur (f)	*koo-lurr*
comb	peigne (m)	*pain*
(to) come	venir	*vuh-neer*
I come	je viens	*zhuh v'yen*
you come	vous venez	*voo vuh-nay*
he comes	il vient	*eel v'yen*
she comes	elle vient	*el v'yen*
we come	nous venons	*noo vuh-nohn*
they (m) come	ils viennent	*eel v'yen*
they (f) come	elles viennent	*el v'yen*
Come!	Venez!	*vuh-nay!*
Come in!	Entrez!	*ahn-tray!*
(to) come back	revenir	*ruh-vuh-neer*
company	compagnie (f)	*kohn-pah-nyee*
complete	complet, -ète	*kohn-play, -plait*
computer	ordinateur (m)	*or-dee-na-turr*
concert	concert (m)	*kohn-sair*
congratulations	félicitations (f)	*fay-lee-see-tahss-yohn*
(to) continue	continuer	*kohn-tee-nway*
conversation	conversation (f)	*kohn-vair-sas-yohn.*
cook	cuisinier (m), -ière (f)	*kwee-zeen-yay, -yair*
(to) cook	faire la cuisine	*'fair la kwee-zeen*

cool	frais, fraîche	*fray, fraish*
copy	copie (f)	*ko-pee*
corkscrew	tire-bouchon (m)	*teer-boo-shohn*
corner	coin (m)	*kwen*
correct	exact, -e	*ek-zakt*
(to) cost	coûter	*koo-tay*
cotton	coton (m)	*ko-tohn*
cough	toux (f)	*too*
country	pays (m)	*pay-ee*
cousin	(m) cousin, -e	*koo-zen, -zeen*
cow	vache (f)	*vash*
crab	crabe (m)	*krahb*
crazy	fou, folle	*foo, fol*
cream	crème (f)	*kraym*
(to) cross	traverser	*tra-vair-say*
crossroads	carrefour (m)	*car-foor*
cup	tasse (f)	*tahss*
customs	douane (f)	*doo-ahn*
(to) cut	couper	*koo-pay*

D

(to) dance	danser	*dahn-say*
dangerous	dangereux, -reuse	*dahn-zhuh-ruh, -ruhz*

dark	sombre	*sohnbr'*
darling	chéri, -e	*shay-ree*
date (of month)	date (f)	*daht*
daughter	fille (f)	*fee*
daughter-in-law	belle-fille (f)	*bell-fee*
day	jour (m)	*zhoor*
dead	mort, -e	*mor, mort*
dear	cher, chère	*shair*
December	décembre (m)	*day-sahnbr'*
(to) decide	décider	*day-see-day*
deep	profond, -e	*pro-fohn, -fohnd*
delay	retard (m)	*ruh-tar*
delighted	enchanté, -e	*ahn-shahn-tay*
delicious	délicieux, -ieuse	*day-lees-yuh, -yuhz*
dentist	dentiste (m)	*dahn-teest*
department store	grand magasin (m)	*grahn ma-ga-zen*
desk	bureau (m)	*bü-ro*
detour	détour (m)	*day-toor*
devil	diable (m)	*d'yahbl'*
dictionary	dictionnaire (m)	*deeks-yo-nair*
different	différent, -e	*dee-fay-rahn, rahnt*
difficult	difficile	*dee-fee-seel*
(to) dine	dîner	*dee-nay*

dining room	salle à manger (f)	*sahl-ah-mahn-zhay*
dinner	dîner (m)	*dee-nay*
direction	direction (f)	*dee-reks-yohn*
dirty	sale	*sahl*
disappointed	déçu, -e	*day-sǔ*
discount	réduction	*ray-dǔks-yohn*
divorced	divorcé, -e	*dee-vor-say*
dizziness	vertige (m)	*vair-teezh*
(to) do	faire	*fair*

"Do" is not used as an auxiliary for asking questions or for the negative. To ask questions simply put the subject after the verb, or use *Est-ce que.* "Do you want . . ." is *Voulez-vous . . .*or *Est-ce que vous voulez . . . .* For negatives, use *ne* and *pas* around the verb. "I don't want" is *Je ne veux pas.*

Don't do that!	Ne faites pas cela!	*nuh fet pah suh-lal*
dock	quai (m)	*kay*
doctor	docteur (m)	*dohk-turr*
dog	chien	*sh'yen*
dollar	dollar (m)	*doh-lahr*
door	porte (f)	*port*
down, downstairs	en bas	*ahn ba*
downtown	en ville	*ahn veel*
dress	robe (f)	*rohb*
(to) drink	boire	*bwahr*

(to) drive	conduire	*kohn-dweer*
driver	conducteur (m)	*kohn-dŭk-turr*
driver's license	permis de conduire (m)	*pair-me duh kohn-dweer*
drum	tambour (m)	*tahn-boor*
drunk	ivre	*eevr'*
dry cleaner	teinturier (m)	*ten-tur-yay*
duck	canard (m)	*ka-nahr*

E

each	chaque	*shahk*
ear	oreille (f)	*oh-ray*
early	de bonne heure	*duh bunn urr*
(to) earn	gagner	*gahn-yay*
earth	terre (f)	*tair*
east	est (m)	*est*
easy	facile	*fa-seel*
(to) eat	manger	*mahn-zhay*
eggs	des oeufs (m. pl)	*day zuh*
eight	huit	*weet*
eighteen	dix-huit	*dee-zweet*
eighty	quatre-vingts	*katr'-ven*
either one	n'importe lequel	*nen-port luh-kel*
elbow	coude (m)	*kood*

electricity	électricité (f)	*ay-lek-tree-see-tay*
elephant	éléphant (m)	*ay-lay-fahн*
elevator	ascenseur (m)	*ah-sahн-surr*
else	autre	*ohtr'*
embassy	ambassade (f)	*ahн-ba-sahd*
emergency	urgence (f)	*ũr-zhahнss*
employee	employé (m)	*ahн-plwa-yay*
end	fin (f)	*feн*
(to) end	finir	*fee-neer*
England	Angleterre	*ahн-gluh-tair*
English	anglais, -e	*ahн-glay, -glaiz*
entertaining	amusant, -e	*a-mũ-zahн, -zahнt*
error	erreur (f)	*ay-rurr*
European	européen, -enne	*uh-ro-pay-eн, -en*
even	même	*mem*
evening	soir (m)	*swahr*
ever	jamais	*zha-may*
every	chaque	*shahk*
everybody	tout le monde	*tool-mohнd*
everything	·tout	*too*
exactly	exactement	*ek-zak-tuh-mahн*
excellent	excellent, -lente	*ek-say-lahн, -lahнt*
except	sauf	*sohf*
(to) exchange	échanger	*ay-shahн-zhay*

Excuse me!	Excusez-moi!	*ex-kü-zay-mwa!*
exit	sortie (f)	*sor-tee*
expensive	cher, chère	*shair*
experience	expérience (f)	*ex-pair-yahns*
explanation	explication (f)	*ex-plee-kass-yohn*
(to) export	exporter	*ex-por-tay*
extra	extra	*ex-tra*
eye	oeil (m)	*oy*

F

face	visage (m)	*vee-zahzh*
factory	usine (f)	*ü-zeen*
fall	chute (f)	*shüte*
(to) fall	tomber	*tohn-bay*
family	famille (f)	*fa-mee*
famous	fameux, -euse	*fa-muh, -muhz*
far	loin	*lwen*
How far?	A quelle distance?	*ah kel dees-tahnss?*
fare	prix (m)	*pree*
farm	ferme (f)	*fairm*
farther	plus loin	*plü lwen ·*
fast	vite	*veet*
fat	gros, grosse	*gro, grohss*
father	père (m)	*pair*

February	février (m)	*fay-vree-ay*
(to) feel	(se) sentir	*(suh) sahн-teer*
How do you feel?	Comment vous sentez-vous?	*ko-mahн voo sahн-tay-voo?*
fever	fièvre (f)	*f'yevr'*
(a) few	quelques	*kel-kuh*
fifteen	quinze	*keнz*
fifty	cinquante	*seнk-ahнt*
(to) fight	se battre	*suh batr'*
(to) fill	remplir	*rahн-pleer*
film	film (m)	*feelm*
finally	enfin	*ahн-feн*
(to) find	trouver	*troo-vay*
finger	doigt (m)	*dwa*
(to) finish	finir	*fee-neer*
finished	fini, -e	*fee-nee*
fire	feu (m)	*fuh*
first	premier, -ère	*pruh-m'yay, -m'yair*
fish	poisson (m)	*pwa-sohн*
(to) fish	pêcher	*pay-shay*
five	cinq	*seнk*
flight	vol (m)	*vohl*
floor	plancher (m)	*plahн-shay*
flower	fleur (f)	*flurr*
(to) fly	voler	*vo-lay*

fly (insect)	mouche (f)	*moosh*
food	alimentation (f)	*ah-lee-mahn-tahs-yohn*
foot	pied (m)	*p'yay*
for	pour	*poor*
foreigner	étranger (m), -gère	*ay-trahn-zhay, -zhair*
forest	forêt (f)	*fo-ray*
(to) forget	oublier	*oo-blee-ay*
Don't forget!	N'oubliez pas!	*noo-blee-ay pal*
fork	fourchette (f)	*foor-shet*
forty	quarante	*ka-rahnt*
fountain	fontaine (f)	*fohn-taine*
four	quatre	*kahtr'*
fourteen	quatorze	*ka-torz*
fox	renard (m)	*ruh-nahr*
France	France (f)	*frahnss*
free	libre	*leebr'*
French	français, -çaise	*frahn-say, -saiz*
fresh	frais, fraîche	*fray, fraish*
Friday	vendredi	*vahn-druh-dee*
fried	frit, frite	*free, freet*
friend	ami (m), -e (f)	*ah-mee*
frog	grenouille (f)	*gruh-noo'ee*
from	de	*duh*

(in) front (of)	en face de	*ahn fahss duh*
fruit	fruit (m)	*frwee*
full	complet, -plète	*kohn-play, -plett*
funny	drôle	*drohl*
furniture	meubles (m)	*muhbl'*
future	futur (m)	*fü-tür*

G

game	jeu (m)	*zhuh*
garden	jardin (m)	*zhahr-den*
gasoline	essence (f)	*ay-sahnss*
gas station	poste d'essence (m)	*post day-sahnss*
garage	garage (m)	*ga-razh*
general	général	*zhay-nay-rahl*
gentleman	monsieur (m)	*muss-yuh*
German	allemand, -e	*ahl-mahn, -mahnd*
Germany	Allemagne	*ahl-mine*
(to) get (obtain)	obtenir	*ob-tuh-neer*
(to) get (become)	devenir	*duh-vuh-neer*
(to) get off	descendre	*day-sahndr'*
(to) get on	monter	*mohn-tay*
(to) get out	sortir	*sor-teer*
Get out!	Sortez!	*sor-tay!*

gift	cadeau (m)	*ka-doh*
(to) give	donner	*doh-nay*
Give me ...	Donnez-moi ...	*doh-nay-mwa*
girl	fille (f)	*fee.*
glass	verre (m)	*vair*
glasses	lunettes (f. pl)	*lü-net*
glove	gant (m)	*gahn*
(to) go	aller	*ah-lay*
I go	je vais	*zhuh vay*
you go	vous allez	*voo za-lay*
he goes	il va	*eel va*
she goes	elle va	*el va*
we go	nous allons	*noo za-lohn*
they (m) go	ils vont	*eel vohn*
they (f) go	elles vont	*el vohn*
(to) go away	s'en aller	*sahn na-lay*
Go away!	Allez-vous en!	*ah-lay-voo zahn!*
(to) go back	revenir	*ruh-vuh-neer*
(to) go on	continuer	*kohn-tee-nway*
Go on!	Continuez!	*kohn-tee-nway!*
goat	chèvre (f)	*shevr'*
God	Dieu (m)	*dyuh*
gold	or (m)	*or*
golf	golf (m)	*gohlf*

good	bon, bonne	*bohn, bunn*
goodbye	au revoir	*ohr-vwahr*
government	gouvernement (m)	*goo-vair-nuh-mahn*
grandfather	grand-père (m)	*grahn-pair*
grandmother	grand-mère (f)	*grahn-mair*
grapes	raisins (m. pl)	*ray-zen*
grateful	reconnaissant, -e	*ruh-ko-nay-sahn,-sahnt*
gray	gris, grise	*gree, greez*
Great!	Formidable!	*for-mee-dahbl'!*
a great many	beaucoup de	*bo-koo-duh*
Greece	Grèce (f)	*gress*
Greek	grec, greque	*grek*
green	vert, verte	*vair, vairt*
group	groupe (m)	*groop*
guide	guide (m)	*gheed*
guitar	guitare (f)	*ghee-tar*

H

had (past participle)	eu	*ŭ*
I had	j'ai eu	*zhay ŭ*
you had	vous avez eu	*voo za-vay zŭ*
hair	cheveux (m. pl.)	*shuh-vuh*

hairbrush	brosse à cheveux (f)	*bross ah shuh-vuh*
haircut	coupe de cheveux (f)	*koop duh shuh-vuh*
half	demi, -e	*duh-mee*
hand	main (f)	*men*
happy	heureux, -reuse	*huh-ruh, -ruhz*
hard	dur, -e	*dŭr*
hat	chapeau (m)	*sha-po*
(to) have	avoir	*ah-vwahr*
I have	j'ai	*zhay*
you have	vous avez	*voo za-vay*
he has	il a	*eel ah*
she has	elle a	*el ah*
we have	nous avons	*noo za-vohn*
they (m) have	ils ont	*eel zohn*
they (f) have	elles ont	*el zohn*
Have you?	Avez-vous?	*ah-vay-voo?*
he	il	*eel*
head	tête (f)	*tet*
heart	coeur (m)	*kurr*
heavy	lourd, lourde	*loor, loord*
(to) hear	entendre	*ahn-tahndr'*
Hello!	Allô!	*ah-lo!*
(to) help	aider	*ay-day*
Help!	Au secours!	*oh suh-koor!*

her (dir. object)	la	*la*
(to) her	lui	*lwee*
her (possessive adj.)	son, sa, ses	*sohn, sa, say*
hers (pronoun)	le sien, la sienne	*luh s'yen, la s'yen*
	les siens, les siennes	*lay s'yen, lay s'yen*
here	ici	*ee-see*
high	haut, -e	*oh, oht*
highway	route (f)	*root*
hill	colline (f)	*ko-leen*
him	le	*luh*
(to) him	lui	*lwee*
his (adj.)	son, sa, ses	*sohn, sa, say*
his (pronoun)	le sien, la sienne	*luh s'yen, la s'yen*
	les siens, les siennes	*lay s'yen, lay s'yen*
history	histoire (f)	*ees-twahr*
home		
(at my) home	chez moi	*shay mwa*
(at) home	à la maison	*ah la may-zohn*
horse	cheval (m)	*shuh-vahl*
hospital	hôpital (m)	*oh-pee-tahl*
hot	chaud, -e	*sho, shohd*
hotel	hôtel (m)	*o-tel*
hour	heure (f)	*urr*

house	maison (f)	*may-zohn*
how	comment	*ko-mahn*
however	pourtant	*poor-tahn*
hundred	cent (m)	*sahn*
(to be) hungry	avoir faim	*ah-vwarh fen*
(to be in a) hurry	être pressé	*.etr' pray-say*
Hurry. up!	Dépêchez-vous!	*day-pay-shay-voo!*
husband	mari (m)	*ma-ree*

I

I	je	*zhuh*
ice	glace (f)	*glahss*
ice cream	glace (f)	*glahss*
idea	idée (f)	*ee-day*
idiot	idiot (m), idiote (f)	*eed-yo, -yot*
if	si	*see*
ill	malade	*ma-lahd*
(to) import	importer	*en-por-tay*
important	important, -e	*en-por-tahn, -tahnt*
impossible	impossible	*en-po-seebl'*
in	dans	*dahn*
included	inclus, -e	*en-klŭ, -klŭz*

industry	industrie (f)	*en-dûs-tree*
information	renseigne-ment (m)	*rahn-sain-yuh-mahn*
inhabitant	habitant (m), -e (f)	*ah-bee-tahn, -tahnt*
inn	auberge (f)	*oh-bairzh*
instead of	au lieu de	*oh lyuh duh*
inside	à l'intérieur	*ah-len-tair-yuhr*
intelligent	intelligent, -e	*en-tay-lee-zhahn, -zhant*
(I am) interested!	Cela m'intéresse!	*suh-la men-tay-ress!*
interesting	intéressant, -e	*en-tay-ray-sahn, -sahnt*
interpreter	interprète (f)	*en-tair-prett*
into	dans	*dahn*
(to) introduce	présenter	*pray-zahn-tay*
invitation	invitation (f)	*en-vee-tass-yohn*
Ireland	Irlande (f)	*eer-lahnd*
Irish	irlandais, -e	*eer-lahn-day, -dayz*
is	est	*ay*
island	ile (f)	*eel*
Israel	Israël	*eess-ra-el*
Israeli	israélien, -ienne	*eess-ra-ail-yen, -yen*
it	il, elle	*eel, el*
its	son, sa, ses	*sohn, sa, say*

| Italian | italien, -ne | *ee-tal-yen, -yen* |
| Italy | Italie | *ee-ta-lee* |

J

jacket	veste (f)	*vest*
jail	prison (f)	*pree-zohn*
January	janvier (m)	*zhahn-vyay*
Japan	Japon (m	*zha-pohn*
Japanese	japonais, -e	*zha-po-nay, -ayz*
jewelry	bijouterie (f)	*bee-zhoot-ree*
Jew, Jewish	juif, juive	*zhweef, zhweev*
job	travail (m)	*tra-vye*
joke	plaisanterie (f)	*play-zahn-tree*
July	juillet (m)	*zhwee-yay*
June	juin (m)	*zhwen*
just	exactement	*ek-zak-tuh-mahn*

K

(to) keep	garder	*gar-day*
Keep out!	Défense d'entrer!	*day-fahns dahn-tray!*
Keep quiet!	Silence!	*see-lahns!*
key	clé(f)	*klay*
kind	sorte (f)	*sort*
king (m)	roi (m)	*rwah*

(to) kiss	embrasser	*ahn-l ra-say*
kitchen	cuisine (f)	*kwee-zeen*
knee	genou (m)	*zhuh-noo*
knife	couteau (m)	*koo-toh*
know		
(to) have knowledge	savoir	*sa-vwahr*
(to) be acquainted with	connaître	*ko-naytr'*
Do you know (something)?	Savez-vous . . . ?	*sa-vay-voo . . . ?*
Do you know (someone)?	Connaissez-vous . . . ?	*ko-nay-say-voo . . . ?*
Who knows?	Qui sait?	*kee say?*

L

ladies' room	toilettes (f. pl.)	*twa-let*
lady	dame (f)	*dahm*
lake	lac (m)	*lahk*
lamb	agneau (m)	*ahn-yo*
land	terre (f)	*tair*
language	langue (f)	*lahng*
large	grand, -e	*grahn, grahnd*
last	dernier, -ère	*dairn-yay, -yair*
late	tard	*tar*
later	plus tard	*plŭ tar*

lawyer	avocat (m. or f.)	*ah-vo-ka*
(to) learn	apprendre	*ah-prahஈdr'*
leather	cuir (m)	*kweer*
(to leave)	partir	*par-teer*
left	gauche	*gohsh*
leg	jambe (f)	*zhahஈb*
lemon	citron (m)	*see-trohஈ*
(to) lend	prêter	*pray-tay*
less	moins	*mweஈ*
lesson	leçon (f)	*luh-sohஈ*

let's: Use the present tense verb form ending in *-ons* (the form that goes with the pronoun *nous*) by itself to express the idea of "Let's (do something)."

Let's go!	Partons!	*par-tohஈ!*
Let's wait a little.	Attendons un peu.	*ah-tahஈ-dohஈ zuஈ puh.*
letter	lettre (f)	*letr'*
lettuce	laitue (f)·	*lay-tü*
liberty	liberté (f)	*lee-bair-tay*
lieutenant	lieutenant. (m)	*l'yuht-nahஈ*
life	vie (f)	*vee*
light	lumière (f)	*lüme-yair*
like	comme	*kom*
Like this.	Comme çal	*kom-sa!*
· (to) like	aimer	*ay-may*

linen	linge (m)	*lanzh*
lion	lion (m)	*l'yohn*
lip	lèvre (f)	*laivr'*
list	liste (f)	*leest*
(to) listen	écouter	*ay-koo-tay*
Listen!	Écoutez!	*ay-koo-tay!*
little (small)	petit, -e	*puh-tee, -teet*
a little	un peu	*un puh*
(to) live	vivre	*veevr'*
living room	salon (m)	*sa-lohn*
lobster	homard (m)	*o-mar*
long	long, longue	*lohn, lohng*
(to) look	regarder	*ruh-gar-day*
Look!	Regardez!	*ruh-gar-day!*
Look out!	Attention!	*ah-tahnss-yohn!*
(to) lose	perdre	*pairdr'*
lost	perdu	*pair-dû*
(a) lot	beaucoup	*bo-koo*
(to) love	aimer	*ay-may*
low	bas, -se	*ba, bahss*
luck	chance	*shahnss*
Good luck!	Bonne chance!	*bunn shahnss!*
luggage	bagage (m)	*ba-gahzh*
lunch	déjeuner (m)	*day-zhuh-nay*

M

machine	machine (f)	*ma-sheen*
madam	madame (f)	*ma-dahm*
made	fait, -e	*fay, fett*
maid	bonne (f)	*bunn*
mailbox	boîte aux lettres (f)	*bwaht oh letr'*
(to) make	faire	*fair*
man	homme (m)	*ohm*
manager	directeur (m)	*dee-rek-turr*
many	beaucoup	*bo-koo*
map	carte (f)	*kart*
March	mars (m)	*marss*
market	marché	*mar-shay*
married	marié, -e	*mar-yay*
mass	messe (f)	*mess*
matches	allumettes (f. pl.)	*ah-lǔ-met*
matter	sujet (m)	*sǔ-zhay*
What's the matter?	Qu'est qu'il y a?	*kess keel ya?*
It does not matter.	Cela n'a pas d'import- ance	*suh-la na pa den-por-tahnss.*
May I?	Est-ce que je peux?	*ess kuh zhuh puh?*
May	mai (m)	*may*

maybe	peut-être	*puh-tetr'*
me	me, moi	*muh, mwah*
(to) mean	vouloir dire	*voo-lwahr deer*
meat	viande (f)	*vee-ahnd*
mechanic	mécanicien (m)	*may-ka-neess-yen*
medicine	médica-ment (m)	*may-dee-ka-mahn*
Mediterranean	Méditer-rannée (f)	*may-dee-tay-ra-nay*
(to) meet	rencontrer	*rahn-kohn-tray*
meeting	réunion (f)	*ray-ûn-yohn*
member	membre (m)	*mahnbr'*
(to) mend	réparer	*ray-pa-ray*
men's room	toilettes (f. pl.)	*twa-let*
menu	carte (f)	*kart*
message	message (m)	*may-sahzh*
meter	compteur (m)	*kohn-turr*
Mexico	Méxique (m)	*mek-seek*
middle	milieu (m)	*meel-yuh*
mile	mille (m)	*meel*
milk	lait (m)	*lay*
million	million (m)	*meel-yohn*
mine	le mien, la mienne	*luh m'yen,* *la m'yen*
	les miens, les miennes	*lay m'yen,* *lay m'yen*
minister	pasteur (m)	*pahss-turr*

minute	minute (f)	*mee-nŭt*
Miss	Mademoi-selle (f)	*mahd-mwa-zell*
(to) miss	manquer	*mahn-kay*
mistake	erreur (f)	*ay-rurr*
Mr.	Monsieur	*muss-yuh*
misunder-standing	malen-tendu (m)	*ma-lahn-tahn-dŭ*
Mrs.	Madame (f)	*ma-dahm*
model	modèle (m)	*mo-dell*
modern	moderne	*mo-dairn*
moment	moment (m)	*mo-mahn*
Monday	lundi (m)	*lun-dee*
money	argent (m)	*ahr-zhahn*
monkey	singe (m)	*senzh*
month	mois (m)	*mwah*
monument	monument (m)	*mo-nŭ-mahn*
moon	lune (f)	*lŭn*
more	plus	*plŭ*
morning	matin (m)	*ma-ten*
mosquito	moustique (m)	*moos-teek*
most	le plus	*luh plŭ*
mother	mère (f)	*mair*
mother-in-law	belle-mère (f)	*bell-mair*
motor	moteur (m)	*mo-turr*

motorcycle	moto-cyclette (f)	*mo-toh-see-klett*
mountain	montagne (f)	*mohn-tine*
mouth	bouche (f)	*boosh*
mouse	souris (f)	*soo-ree*
movie	film (m)	*feelm*
much	beaucoup	*bo-koo*
museum	musée (m)	*mŭ-zay*
music	musique (f)	*mŭ-zeek*
musician	musicien (m), -cienne (f)	*mŭ-zees-yen, -yen*

must: Use *il faut* with the infinitive of the principal verb.

I must go.	Il faut partir.	*eel fo par-teer.*
We must eat.	Il faut manger.	*eel fo mahn-zhay.*
mustache	moustache (f)	*moos-tash*
mustard	moutarde (f)	*moo-tard*
my	mon, ma, mes	*mohn, ma, may*

N

napkin	serviette (f)	*sairv-yet*
name	nom (m)	*nohn*
narrow	étroit, -e	*ay-trwa, -trwaht*
navy	marine (f)	*ma-reen*
near	près	*pray*
necessary	nécessaire	*nay-say-sair*
neck	cou (m)	*koo*

necktie	cravate (f)	*kra-vaht*
(to) need	avoir besoin de	*ah-vwahr buh-zwen duh*
neighborhood	voisinage (m)	*vwa-zee-nahzh*
nephew	neveu (m)	*nuh-vuh*
nervous	nerveux, -euse	*nair-vuh, -vuhz*
neutral	neutre	*nuhtr'*
never	ne . . . jamais	*nuh . . . zha-may*
Never mind.	Ca n'a pas d'impor- tance.	*sa na pa d'en-por-tahnss.*
new	nouveau, -velle	*noo-vo, noo-vell*
news	nouvelles (f. pl.)	*noo-vell*
New Year	Nouvel An	*noo-vel ahn*
next	prochain, -e	*pro-shen, -shen*
nice	gentil, -ille	*zhahn-tee*
night	nuit (f)	*nwee*
nightclub	cabaret (m)	*ka-ba-ray*
nightgown	chemise de nuit (f)	*shuh-meez duh nwee*
nine	neuf	*nuff*
nineteen	dix-neuf	*deez-nuff*
ninety	quatre-vingt- dix	*ka-truh-ven-dees*
no!	non!	*nohn!*
no (adj.)	pas de . . .	*pa.duh . . .*

no money	pas d'argent	*pa dar-zhahn*
no time	pas de temps	*pa duh tahn*
nobody	(ne) . . . personne	*(nuh) . . . pair-sunn*
noise	bruit (m)	*brwee*
noon	midi	*mee-dee*
normal	normal, -e	*nor-mahl*
north	nord (m)	*nor*
nose	nez (m)	*nay*
not	ne . . . pas	*nuh . . . pa*
I can not	je ne peux pas	*zhuh nuh puh pa*
Not yet.	Pas encore.	*pa zahn-kor*
nothing	rien	*r'yen*
(to) notice	remarquer	*ruh-mar-kay*
noun	nom (m)	*nohn*
November	novembre (m)	*no-vahnbr'*
now	maintenant	*men-tuh-nahn*
nowhere	nulle part	*nül par*
number	nombre (m)	*nohnbr'*
nurse	infirmière (f)	*en-feerm-yair*
nuts	noix	*nwa*

O

occasionally	à l'occasion	*ah lo-kaz-yohn*
occupied	occupé	*oh-kü-pay*

| ocean | océan (m) | *oh-say-ahn* |
| o'clock | heure, -s (f) | *urr* |

(See page 33 for use.)

October	octobre (m)	*ok-tobr'*
of	de	*duh*
(to) offer	offrir	*o-freer*
office	bureau (m)	*bû-ro*
officer	officier (m)	*o-fees-yay*
often	souvent	*soo-vahn*
oil	huile (f)	*weel*
o.k.	d'accord	*da-kor*
old	vieux, vieille	*v'yuh, v'yay*
olive	olive (f)	*o-leev*
omelet	omelette (f)	*om-let*
on	sur	*sûr*
once	une fois	*ûne fwa*
At once!	Tout de suite!	*toot sweet!*
one	un, une	*un, ûne*
one way (traffic)	sens unique	*sahns zû-neek*
on time	à l'heure.	*ah lurr*
onion	oignon	*on-yohn*
only	seulement	*suhl-mahn*
open	ouvert, -e	*oo-vair, -vairt*
(to) open	ouvrir	*oo-vreer*
open air	plein air (m)	*plen nair*

opera	opéra (m)	*oh-pay-ra*
opinion	opinion (f)	*oh-peen-yohℵ*
in my opinion	à mon avis	*ah mohℵ na-vee*
opportunity	occasion (f)	*oh-kaz-yohℵ*
opposite	en face	*ahℵ fahss*
or	ou	*oo*
orange	orange	*o-rahℵzh*
orchestra	orchestre (m)	*or-kestr'*
order	ordre (m)	*ordr'*
(to) order	commander	*ko-mahℵ-day*
in order to	afin de	*ah-feℵ duh*
original	original, -e	*oh-ree-zhee-nahl*
other	autre	*ohtr'*
ought	devoir	*duh-vwahr*
you ought to . . .	Vous devriez . . .	*voo duh-vree-yay . . .*

See "should" for complete list of forms.

our	notre	*notr'*
outside	à l'extérieur	*ah lex-tair-yurr*
over (above)	au-dessus	*ohd-sû*
over (finished)	fini, -e	*fee-nee*
overcoat	manteau (m)	*mahℵ-toh*
over there	là-bas,	*la-ba*
overweight	trop lourd, -e	*tro loor, loord*
(to) owe	devoir	*duh-vwahr*

own	propre	*prohpr'*
owner	propriétaire (m)	*pro-pree-yay-tair*
ox, oxen	boeuf, boeufs	*buhf, buh*
oyster	huître (f)	*weetr'*

P

package	paquet (m)	*pa-kay*
paid	payé, -e	*pay-yay*
pain	douleur (f)	*doo-lurr*
(to) paint	peindre	*peɴdr'*
painting	peinture (f)	*peɴ-tûr*
palace	palais (m)	*pa-lay*
pan	casserole (f)	*kass-roll*
paper	papier (m)	*pap-yay*
parade	défilé (m)	*day-fee-lay*
Pardon me!	Excusez-moi!	*ex-kû-zay-mwal*
Parisian	Parisien, -ne	*pa-rees-yeɴ, -yen*
(to) park	parquer	*par-kay*
park	parc (m)	*park*
parents	parents (m. pl)	*pa-rahɴ*
part	partie (f)	*par-tee*
participle	participe (m)	*par-tee-seep*
partner	associé (m)	*ah-sohss-yay*

party (entertainment)	partie	*par-tee*
party (political)	parti (m)	*par-tee*
passenger (train, bus)	voyageur (m), -euse (f)	*vwa-ya-zhurr, -zhuhz*
passenger boat, plane)	passager (m), -ère (f)	*pa-sa-zhay, -zhair*
passport	passeport (m)	*pass-por*
past	passé, -e	*pa-say*
(to) pay	payer	*pay-yay*
peace	paix	*pay*
pen	stylo (m)	*stee-lo*
pencil	crayon (m)	*kray-yohn*
people	des gens (f. pl)	*day zhahn*
percent	pourcentage (m)	*poor-sahn-tazh*
perfect	parfait, -e	*par-fay, -fait*
perfume	parfum (m)	*par-fen*
perhaps	peut-être	*puh-tetr'*
permanent	permanent, -e	*pair-ma-nahn, -nahnt*
permitted	permis, -e	*pair-mee, -meez*
person	personne (f)	*pair-sunn*
phone	téléphone (m)	*tay-lay-fohn*
photo	photo (f)	*fo-toh*
piano	piano (m)	*pee-ah-no*
(to) pick up	ramasser	*ra-ma-say*

picture	tableau (m)	ta-blo
piece	morceau (m)	mor-so
pier	quai (m)	kay
pill	pilule (f)	pee-lùl
pillow	oreiller	o-ray-yay
pin	épingle (f)	ay-pengl'
pink	rose	rohz
pipe (smoking)	pipe (f)	peep
place	endroit (m)	ahn-drwa
plain	simple	senpl'
plans	projets (m. pl)	pro-zhay
plane	avion (m)	ahv-yohn
planet	planète (f)	pla-net
plant (botanical)	plante (f)	plahnt
plant (factory)	usine (f)	ù-zeen
plate	assiette (f)	ahss-yet
play (theater)	pièce (f)	p'yess
(to) play	jouer	zhoo-ay
plastic	plastique (f)	plahss-teek
pleasant	agréable	ah-gray-abl'
please	s'il vous plaît	seel voo play
pleasure	plaisir (m)	play-zeer
plural	pluriel (m)	plùr-yell
pocket	poche (f)	pohsh
poetry	poésie (f)	po-ay-zee

(to) point	indiquer	*en-dee-kay*
police	police (f)	*po-leess*
policeman	agent de police (m)	*ah-zhahn duh po-leess*
poisonous	vénéneux, -neuse	*vay-nay-nuh, -nuhz*
police station	commissariat de police (m)	*ko-mee-sahr-ya duh po-leess*
polite	poli, -e	*po-lee*
poor	pauvre	*pohvr'*
pope	pape (m)	*pahp*
popular	populaire	*po-pü-lair*
pork	porc (m)	*por*
Portugal	Portugal (m)	*por-tü-gahl*
possible	possible	*po-seebl'*
post card	carte postale (f)	*kart pohs-tahl*
post office	bureau de poste (m)	*bü-ro duh post*
potato	pomme de terre (f)	*pom duh tair*
pound (weight)	livre (f)	*leevr'*
(to) practice	pratiquer	*pra-tee-kay*
(to) prefer	préférer	*pray-fay-ray*
pregnant	enceinte	*ahn-sent*
(to) prepare	préparer	*pray-pa-ray*
present (time)	présent (m)	*pray-zahn*
present (gift)	cadeau (m)	*ka-do*

president	président (m)	*pray-zee-dahn*
(to) press	repasser	*ruh-pa-say*
pretty	joli, -e	*zho-lee*
(to) prevent	empêcher	*ahn-pay-shay*
previously	antérieurement	*ahn-tair-yurr-mahn*
price	prix (m)	*pree*
priest	prêtre (m)	*pretr'*
prince	prince (m)	*prenss*
princess	princesse (f)	*pren-sess*
principal	principal, -e	*pren-see-pahl*
prison	prison (f)	*pree-zohn*
private	privé, -e	*pree-vay*
probably	probablement	*pro-ba-bluh-mahn*
problem	problème (m)	*pro-blaym*
production	production (f)	*pro-dŭks-yohn*
profession	profession (f)	*pro-fess-yohn*
professor	professeur (m)	*pro-fay-surr*
program	programme (m)	*prograhm*
(to) promise	promettre	*pro-mettr'*
promised	promis, -e	*pro-mee, -meez*
pronoun	pronom (m)	*pro-nohn*
propaganda	propagande (f)	*pro-pa-gahnd*
property	propriété (f)	*pro-pree-ay-tay*
Protestant	Protestant, -e	*pro-tess-tahn, -tahnt*

public	public, -que	*pŭ-bleek*
publicity	publicité (f)	*pŭ-blee-see-tay*
publisher	éditeur (m)	*ay-dee-turr*
(to) pull	tirer	*tee-ray*
pure	pur, -e	*pŭr*
(to) purchase	acheter	*ash-tay*
purple	violet, -te	*vee-oh-lay, -let*
purse	sac (m)	*sak*
(to) push	pousser	*poo-say*
(to) put	mettre	*mettr'*
(to) put on	mettre	*mettr'*

Q

quality	qualité (f)	*ka-lee-tay*
queen	reine (f)	*ren*
question	question (f)	*kess-t'yohn*
quick	rapide	*ra-peed*
quickly	vite	*veet*
quiet	calme	*kahlm*
quite	tout à fait	*too ta fay*

R

rabbi	rabin (m)	*ra-ben*
rabbit	lapin (m)	*la-pen*
race (contest)	course (f)	*koorss*

radio	radio (f)	*rad-yo*
railroad	chemin de fer (m)	*shuh-men duh fair*
rain	pluie (f)	*plwee*
It's raining.	Il pleut.	*eel pluh.*
raincoat	imperméable (m)	*en-pair-may-ahbl'*
rapidly	rapidement	*ra-peed-mahn*
rarely	rarement	*rahr-mahn*
rate	taux (m)	*toh*
rather	de préférence	*duh pray-fay-rahnss*
I would rather.	J'aimerais mieux.	*zhaim-ray m'yuh.*
razor	rasoir (m)	*ra-zwahr*
(to) read	lire	*leer*
ready	prêt, -e	*pray, prett*
really	vraiment	*vray-mahn*
reason	raison (f)	*ray-zohn*
receipt	reçu (m)	*ruh-sǔ*
(to) receive	recevoir	*ruh-suh-vwahr*
recently	récemment	*ray-sa-mahn*
recipe	recette (f)	*ruh-set*
(to) recognize	reconnaître	*ruh-ko-naitr'*
(to) recommend	recommander	*ruh-ko-mahn-day*
red	rouge	*roozh*
refrigerator	réfrigérateur (m)	*ray-free-zhay-ra-turr*

(to) refuse	refuser	*ruh-fü-zay*
(My) regards to . . .	Mes respects à . . .	*may rais-pay ah . . .*
regular	régulier, -ère	*ray-gül-yay, -yair*
religion	religion (f)	*ruh-leezh-yohn*
(to) remain	rester	*ress-tay*
(to) remember	se rappeler	*suh rap-lay*
(to) rent	louer	*lway*
(to) repair	réparer	*ray-pa-ray*
(to) repeat	répéter	*ray-pay-tay*
Repeat, please!	Répétez, s'il vous plaît!	*ray-pay-tay, seel voo play!*
report	rapport (m)	*ra-por*
(to) represent	représenter	*ruh-pray-zahn-tay*
representative	représantant, -e	*ruh-pray-zahn-tahn, -tahnt*
responsible	responsable	*res-pohn-sahbl'*
resident	résident, -e	*ray-zee-dahn, -dahnt*
(to) rest	se reposer	*suh ruh-po-say*
restaurant	restaurant (m)	*res-toh-rahn*
(to) return	revenir	*ruh-vuh-neer*
revolution	révolution (f)	*ray-vo-lüss-yohn*
reward	récompense (f)	*ray-kohn-pahns*
rice	riz (m)	*ree*
rich	riche	*reesh*
(to) ride	monter à	*mohn-tay. ah*

right (direction)	droit, droite	*drwah, drwaht*
To the right!	A droite!	*ah. drwaht!*
right (correct)	exact, -e	*ex-zakt*
You are right!	Vous avez raison!	*voo za-vay ray-zohn!*
Right away!	Tout de suite!	*tood-sweet!*
That's right!	C'est vrai!	*say vray!*
ring	bague (f)	*bahg*
riot	bagarre (f)	*ba-gahr*
river	fleuve (m)	*fluhv*
road	route (f)	*root*
roof	toit (m)	*twa*
room	chambre (f)	*shahnbr'*
room service	service de restaurant (m)	*sair-veess duh res-toh-rahn*
round trip	aller retour (m)	*ah-lay ruh-toor*
route	trajet (m)	*tra-zhay*
rug	tapis (m)	*ta-pee*
(to) run	courir	*koo-reer*
Russia	Russie (f)	*rù-see*
Russian	Russe	*rùss*

S

sad	triste	*treest*

safe	sûr, -e	*sûr*
safety pin	épingle an-glaise (f)	*ay-pengl' ahn-glayz*
sailor	marin (m)	*ma-ren*
saint	saint, -e	*sen, sent*
salad	salade (f)	*sa-lahd*
salary	salaire (m)	*sa-lair*
sale	solde	*sold*
same	même	*mem*
Saturday	samedi	*sam-dee*
(to) say	dire	*deer*
scenery	paysage (m)	*pay-ee-zahzh*
school	école (f)	*ay-kol*
scissors	ciseaux (m. pl)	*see-zo*
Scotch	écossais, -e	*ay-ko-say, -sayz*
Scotland	Écosse (f)	*ay-koss*
sea	mer (f)	*mair*
seafood	fruits de mer (m. pl)	*frwee duh mair*
season	saison (f)	*say-zohn*
seat	place (f)	*plahss*
secretary	secrétaire (f)	*suh-kray-tair*
(to) see	voir	*vwahr*
(to) seem	sembler	*sahn-blay*
It seems . . .	On dirait . . .	*ohn dee-ray . . .*
seen	vu	*vû*

seldom	rarement	*rahr-mahκ*
(to) sell	vendre	*vahκdr'*
(to) send	envoyer	*ahκ-vwa-yay*
(to) send for	envoyer chercher	*ahκ-vwa-yay shair-shay*
September	septembre (m)	*sep-tahκbr'*
serious	sérieux, -se	*sair-yuh, -yuhz*
service	service (m)	*sair-veess*
seven	sept	*set*
seventeen	dix-sept	*deess-set*
seventy	soixante-dix	*swa-sahκt-deess*
several	plusieurs	*plŭz-yurr*
shampoo	shampooing (m)	*shahκ-pweκ*
shark	requin (m)	*ruh-keκ*
she	elle	*el*
ship	bateau (m)	*ba-toh*
shirt	chemise (f)	*shuh-meez*
shoe	chaussure (f)	*sho-sŭr*
shop	magasin (m)	*ma-ga-zeκ*
short	court, -e	*koor, koort*

should: Use the appropriate one of the following forms of *devoir* with the infinitive of the principal verb.

I should . . .	je devrais . . .	*zhuh duh-vray . . .*
you should . . .	vous de-vriez . . .	*voo duh-vree-ay . . .*

he should ...	il devrait ...	*eel duh-vray ...*
she should ...	elle de- vrait ...	*el duh-vray ...*
we should ...	nous de- vrions ...	*noo duh-vree-ahn ...*
they (m) should ...	ils de vraient ...	*eel duh-vray ...*
they (f) should ...	elles de- vraient ...	*el duh-vray ...*
I should leave.	Je devrais partir.	*zhuh duh-vray par- teer.*
shoulder	épaule (f)	*ay-pohl*
show	spectacle (m)	*spek-tahkl'*
(to) show	montrer	*mohn-tray*
Show me!	Montrez-moi!	*mohn-tray-mwa!*
shower	douche (f)	*doosh*
shrimps	crevettes (f. pl)	*kruh-vet*
shut	fermé, -e	*fair-may*
(to) shut	fermer	*fair-may*
sick	malade	*ma-lahd*
(to) sign	signer	*seen-yay*
silk	soie (f)	*swa*
silver	argent (m)	*ar-zhahn*
since	depuis	*duh-pwee*
sincerely	sincèrement	*sen-sair-mahn*
(to) sing	chanter	*shahn-tay*

singer	chanteur (m), -e (f)	*shahn-turr, -tuhz*
sir	monsieur (m)	*muss-yuh*
sister	soeur (f)	*surr*
sister-in-law	belle-soeur (f)	*bell-surr*
Sit down!	Asseyez-vous!	*ah-say-yay-voo!*
six	six	*seess*
sixteen	seize	*sayz*
sixty	soixante	*swa-sahnt*
size	taille (f)	*tye*
(to) skate	patiner	*pa-tee-nay*
(to) ski	skier	*skee-yay*
skin	peau (f)	*po*
skirt	jupe (f)	*zhŭp*
sky	ciel (m)	*s'yell*
(to) sleep	dormir	*dor-meer*
sleeve	manche (f)	*mahnsh*
slowly	lentement	*lahnt-mahn*
small	petit, -e	*puh-tee, -teet*
(to) smoke	fumer	*fŭ-may*
snow	neige (f)	*nayzh*
so	donc	*dohnk*
soap	savon (m)	*sa-vohn*
socks	chaussettes (f. pl)	*sho-set*
sofa	canapé (m)	*ka-na-pay*

soft	doux, douce	*doo, dooss*
soldier	soldat (m)	*sol-da*
some (a little)	un peu de	*un puh duh*
somebody	quelqu'un	*kelk-un*
something	quelque chose	*kel-kuh shohz*
sometimes	quelquefois	*kel-kuh-fwah*
somewhere	quelque part	*kel-kuh par*
son	fils (m)	*feess*
son-in-law	beau-fils (m)	*bo-feess*
song	chanson (f)	*shahn-sohn*
soon	bientôt	*b'yen-toh*
(I am) sorry.	Je regrette.	*zhuh ruh-grett*
soup	soupe (f)	*soop*
south	sud (m)	*sùd*
South America	Amérique du Sud	*ah-may-reek dù sùd*
souvenir	souvenir (m)	*soo-vuh-neer*
Spain	Espagne	*ess-pahn-yuh*
Spanish	espagnol, -e	*ess-pan-yohl*
(to) speak	parler	*par-lay*
special	spécial, -e	*spais-yahl*
(to) spend	dépenser	*day-pahn-say*
spoon	cuiller (f)	*kwee-yair*
sport	sport (m)	*spor*
spring	printemps (m)	*pren-tahn*

stairs	escalier (m)	*ess-kahl-yay*
stamp	timbre (m)	*tenbr'*
star	étoile (f)	*ay-twahl*
(to) start	commencer	*ko-mahn-say*
state	état (m)	*ay-ta*
station	gare (f)	*gar*
statue	statue (f)	*sta-tü*
(to) stay	rester	*res-tay*
steak	steak (m)	*stek*
steel	acier (m)	*ass-yay*
steward	steward (m)	*stoo-ward*
stewardess	hôtesse (f)	*o-tess*
still	encore	*ahn-kor*
stockings	bas (m. pl)	*ba*
stone	pierre (f)	*p'yair*
Stop!	Arrêtez!	*ah-ray-tay!*
Stop it!	Assez!	*ah-say!*
store	magasin (m)	*ma-ga-zen*
storm	orage (m)	*o-rahzh*
story	histoire (f)	*ees-twahr*
straight ahead	tout droit	*too drwa*
strange	étrange	*ay-trahnzh*
street	rue (f)	*rü*
string	corde (f)	*kord*
strong	fort, -e	*for, fort*

student	étudiant (m), -e (f)	*ay-tŭd-yahn, -yahnt*
(to) study	étudier	*ay-tŭd-yay*
style	style	*steel*
subway	métro (m)	*may-tro*
suddenly	tout d'un coup	*too dun koo*
suede	suède (m)	*swaid*
sugar	sucre (m)	*sŭkr'*
suit	complet (m)	*kohn-play*
suitcase	valise (f)	*va-leez*
summer	été (m)	*ay-tay*
sun	soleil (m)	*so-lay*
Sunday	dimanche (m)	*dee-mahnsh*
sure	sûr, -e	*sŭr*
surely	sûrement	*sŭr-mahn*
surprise	surprise (f)	*sŭr-preez*
sweater	sweater (m)	*sweater*
sweet	doux, douce	*doo, dooss*
(to) swim	nager	*na-zhay*
swimming pool	piscine (f)	*pee-seen*
swim suit	maillot de bain (m)	*ma-yo duh ben*
Swiss	suisse	*sweess*
Switzerland	Suisse (f)	*sweess*

T

table	table (f)	*tahbl'*

tablecloth	nappe (f)	*nap*
tailor	tailleur (m)	*ta-yurr*
(to) take	prendre	*prahиdr'*
take away	enlever	*ahи-luh-vay*
(to) take care of	prendre soin de	*prahиdr' sweи duh*
take a walk (ride)	faire une promenade	*fair ûne prom-nahd*
(to) talk	parler	*par-lay*
tall	grand, -e	*grahи, grahиd*
tank	réservoir (m)	*ray-zair-vwar*
tape	ruban (m)	*rŭ-bahи*
tape recorder	magnétophone (m)	*man-yay-toh-fohи*
tax	impô (m)	*eи-po*
taxi	taxi (m)	*tak-see*
tea	thé (m)	*tay*
(to) teach	enseigner	*ahи-sayn-yay*
teacher	professeur (m)	*pro-fay-surr*
team	équipe (f)	*ay-keep*
telegram	télégramme (m)	*tay-lay-grahm*
telephone	téléphone (m)	*tay-lay-fohn*
television	télévision (f)	*tay-lay-veez-yohи*
(to) tell	dire	*deer*
Tell me . . .	Dites-moi . . .	*deet-mwa . . .*
Tell him (her) . . .	Dites-lui . . .	*deet-lwee . . .*

temple	temple (m)	*tahnpl'*
temperature	température (f)	*tahn-pay-ra-tŭr*
ten	dix	*deess*
tennis	tennis (m)	*tay-neess*
tense	temps (m)	*tahn*
past tense	temps passé	*tahn pa-say*
future tense	temps futur	*tahn fŭ-tŭr*
terrace	terrasse (f)	*tay-rass*
terrible	terrible	*tay-reebl'*
than	que	*kuh*
thank you	merci	*mair-see*
that	que	*kuh*
the	le, la, les	*luh, la, lay*
theatre	théâtre (m)	*tay-ahtr'*
their	leur, leurs	*lurr*
them (dir. obj.)	les	*lay*
(to) them	eux	*uh*
then	alors	*ah-lor*
there	là	*la*
There is	Il y a	*eel ee ya . . .*
There are . . .		
these	ces, ceux-ci, celles-ci	*say, suh-see, sell-see*
they	ils (m), elles (f)	*eel, ell*
thin	mince	*mens*

thing	chose (f)	*shohz*
(to) think	penser	*pahn-say*
Do you think . . . ?	Pensez-vous . . . ?	*pahn-say-voo . . . ?*
I think . . .	Je pense . . .	*zhuh pahnss . . .*
third	troisième	*trwahz-yem*
(I am) thirsty.	J'ai soif.	*zhay swahf.*
thirteen	treize	*trayz*
thirty	trente	*trahnt*
this	ce, cette, celui-ci, celle-ci	*suh, set, suh-lwee-see, sell-see*
those	ces, ceux-là celles-la	*say, suh-la, sell-la*
thousand	mille	*meel*
thread	fil (m)	*feel*
three	trois	*trwa*
throat	gorge (f)	*gorzh*
through	à travers	*ah tra-vair*
Thursday	jeudi	*zhuh-dee*
ticket	billet (m)	*bee-yay*
tie	cravate (f)	*kra-vaht*
tiger	tigre (m)	*teegr'*
time	temps (m)	*tahn*
tip	pourboire (m)	*poor-bwar*
tire	pneu (m)	*pnuh*

tired	fatigué, -e	*fa-tee-gay*
to (direction)	à	*ah*
to (in order to)	afin de	*ah-fen duh*
toast	toast (m)	*tohst*
tobacco	tabac (m)	*ta-ba*
today	aujourd'hui	*oh-zhoor-dwee*
toe	doigt de pied (m)	*dwa duh p'yay*
together	ensemble	*ahn-sahnbl'*
tomato	tomate (f)	*to-maht*
tomorrow	demain	*duh-men*
tomb	tombe (f)	*tohnb*
tongue	langue (f)	*lahng*
tonight	ce soir (m)	*suh swahr*
too (also)	aussi	*o-see*
too (excessive)	trop	*tro*
tool	outil (m)	*oo-tee*
tooth	dent (f)	*dahn*
toothbrush	brosse à dents	*bross ah dahn*
toothpaste	dentifrice (m)	*dahn-tee-freess*
touring	en visitant	*ahn vee-zee-tan*
tourist	touriste	*too-reest*
toward	vers	*vair*
towel	serviette (f)	*sairv-yet*
tower	tour (f)	*toor*
town	ville (f)	*veel*

toy	jouet (m)	*zhoo-ay*
trade fair	foire (f)	*fwahr*
traffic	circulation (f)	*seer-kŭ-lass-yohn*
train	train (m)	*tren*
translation	traduction (f)	*tra-dŭks-yohn*
(to) travel	voyager	*vwa-ya-zhay*
travel agent	agent de voyage (m)	*ah-zhahn duh vwa-yahzh*
traveler	voyageur (m)	*vwa-ya-zhurr*
treasurer	trésorier (m)	*tray-zohr-yay*
tree	arbre (m)	*ahrbr'*
trip	voyage (m)	*vwa-yahzh*
trouble	difficulté (f)	*dee-fee-kŭl-tay*
trousers	pantalon (m)	*pahn-ta-lohn*
truck	camion (m)	*kam-yohn*
true	vrai, -e	*vray*
truth	vérité (f)	*vay-ree-tay*
(to) try, try on	essayer	*ay-say-yay*
Tuesday	mardi	*mar-dee*
Turkey	Turquie	*tŭr-kee*
Turkish	turque	*tŭrk*
(to) turn	tourner	*toor-nay*
(to) turn off	éteindre	*ay-tendr'*
(to) turn on	allumer	*ah-lŭ-may*
twelve	douze	*dooz*

two	deux	*duh*
typewriter	machine à écrire (f)	*ma-sheen ah ay-kreer*
typical	typique	*tee-peek*

U

ugly	laid, -e	*lay, laid*
umbrella	parapluie (m)	*pa-ra-plwee*
uncle	oncle (m)	*ohⁿkl'*
under	sous	*soo*
underneath	en dessous	*ahⁿ duh-soo*
(to) understand	comprendre	*kohⁿ-prahⁿdr'*
Do you understand?	Comprenez-vous?	*kohⁿ-pruh-nay-voo?*
I don't understand.	Je ne comprends pas.	*zhuh nuh kohⁿ-prahn pa.*
underwear	sous-vête-ment (m)	*soo-vet-mahⁿ*
unfortunately	malheureuse-ment	*ma-luh-ruhz-mahⁿ*
uniform	uniforme (m)	*ŭ-nee-form*
United States	Etats-Unis (m. pl.)	*ay-ta-zŭ-nee*
in the United States	aux Etats-Unis	*oh zay-ta-zŭ-nee*
United Nations	Nations Unies (f. pl.)	*nass-yohⁿ-zŭ-nee*
university	université (f)	*ŭ-nee-vair-see-tay*

until	jusqu'à	*zhůs-ka*
up (upstairs)	en haut	*ahн oh*
Get up!	Levez-vous!	*luh-vay-voo!*
urgent	urgent, -e	*ůr-zhahн, -zhahнt*
us	nous	*noo*
(to) use	employer	*ahн-plwa-yay*
useful	utile	*ů-teel*
usually	d'habitude	*da-bee-tůd*

V

vacant	libre	*leebr'*
(on) vacation	en vacances	*ahн-va-kahнs*
vaccination	vaccination (f)	*vak-see-nass-yohн*
valley	vallée (f)	*va-lay*
valuable	de valeur	*duh va-luhr*
value	valeur (f)	*va-luhr*
vanilla	vanille (f)	*va-nee*
various	divers, -e	*dee-vair, -vairss*
vegetable	légume (m)	*lay-gůme*
verb	verbe (m)	*vairb*
very	très	*tray*
very well	très bien	*tray b'yeн*
view	vue (f)	*vů*
village	village (m)	*vee-lahzh*
vinegar	vinaigre (m)	*vee-naigr'*

visa	visa (m)	*vee-za*
visit	visite (f)	*vee-zeet*
visitor	visiteur (m), -euse (f)	*vee-zee-turr, -tuhz*
(to) visit (a place)	visiter	*vee-zee-tay*
(to) visit (a person)	rendre visite à	*rahndr' vee-zeet ah*
violin	violon (m)	*vee-oh-lohn*
voice	voix (f)	*vwa*
volcano	volcan (m)	*vol-kahn*
voyage	voyage (m)	*vwa-yahzh*

W

waist	taille (f)	*tye*
(to) wait	attendre	*ah-tahndr'*
Wait here!	Attendez ici!	*ah-tahn-day zee-see!*
Waiter!	Garçon!	*gar-sohn!*
Waitress!	Mademoiselle!	*mahd-mwa-zell!*
a waitress	une ser-veuse (f)	*ûne sair-vuhz*
(to) walk	marcher	*mar-shay*
wall	mur	*mûr*
wallet	portefeuille (m)	*port-foy*
(to) want	vouloir	*voo-lwahr*
I want	je veux	*zhuh vuh*
you want	vous voulez	*voo voo-lay*

he wants	il veut	*eel vuh*
she wants	elle veut	*el vuh*
we want	nous voulons	*noo voo-lohn*
they (m) want	ils veulent	*eel vuhl*
they (f) want	elles veulent	*el vuhl*
Do you want . . . ?	Voulez-vous . . . ?	*voo-lay-voo . . . ?*
war	guerre (f)	*gair*
warm	chaud, -e	*shoh, shohd*
(I) was	j'étais	*zhay-tay*
he was	il était	*eel ay-tay*
it was	c'était	*say-tay*
she was	elle était	*el ay-tay*
(to) wash	laver	*la-vay*
watch	montre (f)	*mohntr'*
Watch out!	Faites attention!	*fet ah-tahnss-yohn*
water	eau (f)	*oh*
water color	aquarelle (f)	*ah-kwa-rell*
way	chemin (m)	*shuh-men*
in this way.	de cette manière (f)	*duh set man-yair*
we	nous	*noo*
weak	faible	*faibl'*
(to) wear	porter	*por-tay*
weather	temps (m)	*tahn*

wedding	mariage (m)	*ma-ree-ahzh*
week	semaine (f)	*suh-men*
weekend	week-end	*week-end*
(to) weigh	peser	*puh-zay*
weight	poids (m)	*pwa*
Welcome!	Bienvenue!	*b'yen-vuh-nu!*
(you are) welcome	il n'y a pas de quoi	*eel nee ya pa duh kwa*
well	bien	*b'yen*

went

I went	je suis allé	*zhuh swee za-lay*
you went	vous êtes allé	*voo zett ah-lay*
he went	il est allé	*eel ay ta-lay*
she went	elle est allée	*el ay ta-lay*
we went	nous sommes allés	*noo som za-lay*
they (m) went	ils sont allés	*eel sohn ta-lay*
they (f) went	elles sont allées	*el sohn ta-lay*

were

we were	nous étions	*noo zait-yohn*
you were	vous étiez	*voo zait-yay*
they (m) were	ils étaient	*eel zay-tay*
they (f) were	elles étaient	*el zay-tay*
west	ouest (m)	*west*
what	que	*kuh*
What?	Quoi?	*kwa?*

What's the matter?	Qu'est-ce qu'il y a?	*kess keel ee ya?*
What time is it?	Quelle heure est-il?	*kel urr ay-teel?*
What do you want?	Que voulez-vous?	*kuh voo-lay-voo?*
wheel	roue (f)	*roo*
when	quand	*kahn*
where	où	*oo*
wherever	partout où	*par-too oo*
Where to?	Quelle direction?	*kel dee-reks-yohn?*
whether	si	*see*
which (sub.)	qui	*kee*
which (obj.)	que	*kuh*
while	alors que	*ah-lor kuh*
for a while	pendant un moment	*pahn-dahn tun mo-mahn*
white	blanc, blanche	*blahn, blahnsh*
who	qui	*kee*
whole	entier, -ière	*ahnt-yay, -yair*
whom	que	*kuh*
why	pourquoi	*poor-kwa*
Why not?	Pourquoi pas?	*poor-kwa pa?*
wide	large	*larzh*
widow	veuve (f)	*vuhv*
widower	veuf (m)	*vuhf*

| wife | femme (f) | *fahm* |
| wild | sauvage | *so-vahzh* |

will: The future is formed by adding the appropriate ending to the final *r* of the infinitive: *(je) -ai, (il, elle) -a, (nous) -ons, (vous) -ez, (ils, elles) -ont.* (Or you can express the future idea by using a form of *aller,* "to go," with the infinitive. See p. 143.) Several important common verbs have special forms for the future, but they all have the regular ending: *(être) je serai; (avoir) j'aurai; (aller) j'irai; (venir) je viendrai; (faire) je ferai.*

I will speak	je parlerai	*zhuh par-luh-ray*
Will you finish?	Finirez-vous?	*fee-nee-ray-voo?*
He won't allow it.	Il ne le permettra pas.	*eel nuh luh pair-met-ra pa.*
to win	gagner	*gahn-yay*
wind	vent (m)	*vahn*
window	fenêtre (f)	*fuh-netr'*
wine	vin (m)	*ven*
winter	hiver (m)	*ee-vair*
(to) wish	désirer	*day-zee-ray*
without	sans	*sahn*
wolf	loup (m)	*loo*
woman	femme (f)	*fahm*
wonderful	merveilleux, -se	*mair-vay-yuh, -yuhz*
won't (See "will.")		
wood, woods	bois (m)	*bwa*
wool	laine (f)	*lain*

word	mot (m)	*mo*
work	travail (m)	*tra-vye*
(to) work	travailler	*tra-va-yay*
world	monde (m)	*mohnd*
(Don't) worry!	Ne vous en faites pas!	*nuh voo zahn fait pal*
worse	pire	*peer*

would: Express the idea of "would" by adding the appropriate one of the following endings to the final *r* of the infinitive: *(je) -ais, (il, elle) -ait, (nous) -ions, (vous) -iez, (ils, elles) aient.*

you would write	vous écririez	*voo zay-kreer-yay*
I would like . . .	je voudrais . . .	*zhuh voo-dray . . .*
would you like . . . ?	Voudriez-vous . . . ?	*voo-dree-ay voo . . . ?*
wrist	poignet (m)	*pwahn-yay*
(to) write	écrire	*ay-kreer*
write it.	Écrivez-le.	*ay-kree-vay luh.*
writer	écrivain	*ay-kree-ven.*
wrong	faux, fausse	*fo, fohss*
I am wrong.	J'ai tort.	*zhay tor.*

Y

year	année	*ah-nay*
yellow	jaune	*zhohn*
yes	oui	*wee*

yesterday	hier	*ee-yair*
yet	pourtant	*poor-tahn*
not yet	pas encore	*pa zahn-kor*
you	vous	*voo*
young	jeune	*zhuhn*
your	votre	*votr'*
yours	le vôtre	*luh vohtr'*

Z

zipper	fermeture éclair (f)	*fairm-tŭr ay-klair*
zoo	zoo (m)	*zo*
zone	zone (f)	*zohn*

Point to the Answer

For speedy reference and, when in doubt, to get a clear answer to a question you have just asked, show the following sentence to the person you are addressing and let *him* point to the answer to your question.

Avis aux interlocuteurs: Pour être sûr d'avoir été bien compris je vous prie de montrer la réponse à ma question. Merci.

| Oui. | Non. | Peut-être. |
| Yes. | No. | Perhaps. |

| Certainement. | C'est bien. |
| Certainly. | All right. |

Pardon.
Excuse me.

Je comprends.
I understand.

Je ne comprends pas.
I don't understand.

Qu'est-ce que vous désirez?
What do you want?

Je sais.
I know.

Je ne sais pas.
I don't know.

Encore.
Again *or* more.

Assez.
Enough.

Ouvert.
Open.

Fermé.
Closed.

Trop.
Too much.

Pas assez.
Not enough.

Défense d'entrer.
No admittance.

C'est défendu.
It is forbidden.

Propriété privée.
Private property.

Vous devez partir.
You must leave.

Maintenant.
Now.

Plus tard.
Later.

Trop tôt.
Too early.

Trop tard.
Too late.

Aujourd'hui.
Today.

Demain.
Tomorrow.

Hier.
Yesterday.

Ce soir.
Tonight.

Hier soir.
Last night.

Demain soir.
Tomorrow night.

Cette semaine.
This week.

La semaine passée.
Last week

La semaine prochaine.
Next week.

C'est possible.
It's possible.

Ce n'est pas possible.
It's not possible.

C'est entendu.
It is agreed.

Très bien.
Very good.

Ce n'est pas bien.
It isn't good.

C'est près.
It's near.

Très loin.
Very far.

Trop loin.
Too far.

C'est tout.
That's all.

Ici.
Here.

Là-bas.
Over there.

Tournez à gauche.
Turn left.

Tournez à droite.
Turn right.

Allez tout droit.
Go straight ahead.

Venez avec moi.
Come with me.

Suivez-moi.
Follow me.

Allons.
Let's go.

Nous sommes arrivés.
We have arrived.

Arrêtez ici.
Stop here.

Attendez-moi.
Wait for me.

Je ne peux pas.
I cannot.

J'attendrai.
I will wait.

Je dois partir.
I must go.

Revenez plus tard.
Come back later.

Je reviendrai tout de suite.
I'll be right back.

Il n'est pas ici.
He is not here.

Elle n'est pas ici.
She is not here.

Mon nom est ———.
My name is ———.

Votre nom?
Your name?

Numéro de téléphone?
Telephone number?

Adresse?
Address?

lundi
Monday

mardi
Tuesday

mercredi
Wednesday

jeudi
Thursday

vendredi
Friday

samedi
Saturday

dimanche Sunday	A ——— **heures.** At ——— o'clock.

C'est ——— **francs**
——— **centimes.**
It's ——— francs
——— centimes.

un one	**deux** two	**trois** three
quatre four	**cinq** five	**six** six
sept seven	**huit** eight	**neuf** nine
dix ten	**onze** eleven	**douze** twelve

treize thirteen	**quatorze** fourteen
quinze fifteen	**seize** sixteen
dix-sept seventeen	**dix-huit** eighteen
dix-neuf nineteen	**vingt** twenty
treize thirty	**quarante** forty

fifty cinquante	**soixante** sixty
soixante-dix seventy	**quatre-vingts** eighty
quatre-vingt-dix ninety	**cent** one hundred
mille one thousand	**dix-mille** ten thousand